DISCARD

DATE DUE	
MAR 0 7 2019	

CULTURES OF THE WORLD
CHILE

by Jane Kohen Winter/Susan Roraff

BENCHMARK BOOKS

MARSHALL CAVENDISH
NEW YORK

PICTURE CREDITS
Cover photo: © Wolfgang Kaehler
Steve Bly/Houserstock: 5, 42 • Ricardo Carrasco S.: 135 (both) • Victor Englebert:
20, 24, 34, 49, 85, 89, 92, 96, 110, 118, 121, 123, 124, 126 • Paz Errazuriz: 72 • Peter
Francis/South American Pictures: 17, 26, 31 • Robert Francis/South American Pictures:
9, 10, 11, 22, 53, 58, 59, 90, 107, 114 (both), 115 • Getty Images/Hulton Archive: 46, 48,
99 • Eduardo Gil: 1, 3, 4, 12, 16, 18, 32, 36, 38, 39, 40, 51, 54, 66 (both), 68, 91, 93,
101, 102, 103, 104, 105, 108, 116, 117, 120, 122, 125, 129 • HBL Network Photo Agency:
43, 44, 50, 62, 74, 112 • Jason P. Howe/South American Pictures: 70, 84 • Susan Mann/
South American Pictures: 102 • Marcelo Montecino: 21, 23 (both), 25, 28, 29, 30, 35, 41,
52, 55, 56, 60, 63, 64, 65, 67, 69, 73, 75, 76, 77, 79, 81, 82, 94, 100 • Times Media
Private Limited: 131 • Tony Morrison/South American Pictures: 8, 13, 14, 15, 19, 37, 47,
106 • Tony Perrottet: 57 • Michael J. Pettypool/Houserstock: 6 • UPI/Bettman: 95

ACKNOWLEDGMENTS
With thanks to Delmarie Martinez, Assistant Professor, University of Central Florida,
for her expert reading of the manuscript.

PRECEDING PAGE
Mestizo children from northern Chile.

Marshall Cavendish Corporation
99 White Plains Road
Tarrytown, NY 10591
Website: www.marshallcavendish.com

© 1990, 2002 by Times Media Private Limited
All rights reserved. First edition 1990.
Second edition 2002.

Originated and designed by
Times Books International, an imprint of
Times Media Private Limited, a member of the
Times Publishing Group

Printed in Malaysia

Library of Congress Cataloging-in-Publication Data:
Winter, Jane Kohen, [date]
   Chile / by Jane Kohen Winter, Susan Roraff.—2nd ed.
     p. cm.—(Cultures of the world)
   Includes bibliographical references and index.
   Summary: Introduces the history, geography, culture, and lifestyles of Chile.
   ISBN 0-7614-1360-X
   1. Chile—Juvenile literature. [1. Chile.] I. Roraff, Susan. II. Title. III. Series.
F3058.5 .W56 2002
983—dc21   2001047827

6 5 4 3

CONTENTS

A ranger at Paine National
Park in southern Chile,
one of South America's
newest nature reserves.

**Cures on wheels offered
by a folk medicine seller.**

INTRODUCTION

CHILE HAS A UNIQUE GEOGRAPHY and great natural beauty. This long, narrow country lines South America's western coast from the Peruvian border to the island of Tierra del Fuego. The result is a rich diversity of climates and landscapes: from subtropical to subarctic, from deserts to forests to swamps, and from mountains and volcanoes to lakes. Chile has, in the words of Nobel prize-winning poet Gabriela Mistral, "naked rocks, hard jungle, vast orchards, snows and icebergs last."

Northern Chile is dominated by the Atacama Desert, some parts of which have never received a single drop of rain. Central Chile is known for its pleasant climate and fertile soil, and the south is notorious for its fierce winds, icy temperatures, and rough seas. Chile's western border is on the Pacific Ocean, and in the east rises the stunning Andean mountain range.

Chileans share a common language, religion, and ethnic background. Educated, artistic, and cosmopolitan, Chileans are some of the friendliest and receptive people in Latin America.

GEOGRAPHY

CHILE IS THE LONGEST COUNTRY in the world. Though it stretches 2,700 miles (4,345 km) along the western coast of South America, its average width is only 110 miles (177 km).

The Atacama Desert lies between Chile and Peru in the north. The Andes, covering a third of Chilean land, separate Chile from Argentina and Bolivia in the east. With an area of more than 292,000 square miles (756,277 square km), excluding the disputed Antarctic territory, Chile is a little larger than Texas. The Juan Fernández Islands and Easter Island in the South Pacific Ocean are also part of Chile.

Where Chile got its name remains a mystery, although there are at least six different stories. Some of these stories trace the origin of the name to an Amerindian language. A popular definition of the word "chile" is "land's end." Others believe that the name derives from the call of a bird, "cheele-cheele."

Chile is subject to extremes in weather due to winds, storms, and ocean currents. The country lies in a geologically active zone and is prone to earthquakes and volcanic eruptions. More than 100 earthquakes have been recorded since 1575. These are sometimes followed by tidal waves, or tsunamis. Flash floods caused by the rapid melting of snow in the Andes damage villages often, and fishermen are always on the alert for sudden storms and strong currents. Major cities such as Valparaíso and Concepción have been damaged repeatedly by natural disasters.

Chilean terrain ranges from the dry Atacama Desert in the north to the green Central Valley to the forested Lake District in the south to icy fjords and glaciers at the southernmost tip of the country. Because of Chile's length, daylight hours vary greatly. On the longest day of the year, December 23, Arica in the north sees about 13 hours of daylight, while Puerto Williams in the far south sees 17.

Opposite: **Lake Pehoe at Torres del Paine is a scenic spot of lush natural beauty in Chile.**

After the rain, desert blooms peek through crevices in the hardened mud slabs of the Atacama Desert.

NORTHERN, CENTRAL, AND SOUTHERN CHILE

Chile is divided into three major geographic regions that differ dramatically in terms of population, climate, topography, and natural resources.

Northern Chile ranges from the Peruvian border to the city of La Serena; it includes the bleak, thinly populated Atacama Desert. Northern Chile contains great deposits of nitrates and copper that make an important contribution to the nation's economy.

Central Chile lies between La Serena and Concepción and is the heartland of the country. Some 80 percent of the population live in the major cities of this region. The capital, Santiago has a population of 5.2 million. The twin cities of Valparaíso-Viña del Mar, the second largest port and a resort area, have a combined population of 800,000. The Concepción-Talcahuano metropolitan area has a combined population of 840,000. The central region is green and highly cultivated with a striking resemblance to the central valley of California. From Santiago, snow-capped Andean peaks with some of the world's best ski resorts are only a two-hour drive away, and the beach resort of Viña del Mar is a two-hour drive to the west.

Southern Chile begins south of Concepción and extends all the way to Cape Horn, South America's southernmost point. South of the Bío-Bío River lies Chile's Lake District, which has been likened to the Pacific Northwest of the United States in climate and to Switzerland in terms of scenic grandeur. In Villarrica, a major resort town, an active volcano occasionally pours white-hot lava over its snowcapped peaks, a most unusual sight. The area contains deep-blue lakes, stunning glaciers, and lush forests, making it a prime vacation spot. Many of Chile's German

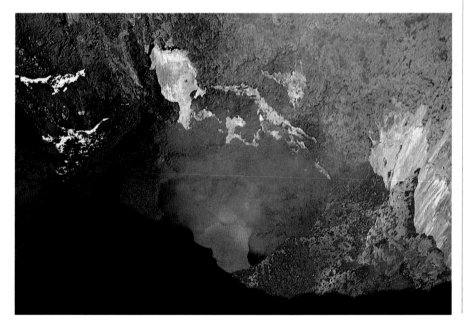

Chile's Lake District is characterized by such topographical features as the 8,809-foot (2,685-m) Volcán Villarrica.

immigrants and most of the remaining indigenous Indians, the Mapuche ("mah-POO-chay"), live in the Lake District.

Southern Chile contains a maze of hundreds of small islands, dramatic fjords, and glaciers. Punta Arenas, the most southerly city, lies on the Strait of Magellan, an important passageway from the Atlantic to the Pacific before the opening of the Panama Canal in 1914. Across the strait lies the island of Tierra del Fuego, or Land of Fire, which is shared with Argentina.

Southern Chile has violent climatic conditions, with terrific storms, freezing rains, and high winds. This is why, although southern Chile occupies more than one-third of the country's land area, it is populated by a small percentage of its people.

"The sense of sublimity, which the…forest-clad mountains of Tierra del Fuego excited in me … has left an indelible impression on my mind."

—Charles Darwin, in Voyage of the Beagle

Right: **In the days before the opening of the Panama Canal, seafarers sailed by Punta Arenas, an important port on the Strait of Magellan named after Ferdinand Magellan, the first European to sail through the strait.**

Opposite: **The snow-capped peak of Volcán Putana dominates the landscape of San Pedro de Atacama.**

THE ANDES AND MOUNTAIN SICKNESS

The single geographic feature that unifies the diverse regions of Chile is the Andean mountain range. Some of Chile's peaks are taller than the highest mountains in Europe, Africa, and the United States. The Ojos del Salado, for instance, is 22,539 feet (6,870 m) tall, 2,219 feet (676 m) taller than Mount McKinley, the tallest mountain in the United States.

Mountain sickness, or *soroche* ("soh-ROH-cheh"), can occur at altitudes of 10,000 feet (3,048 m) and is completely unpredictable in its choice of victims. Trekkers who have never had altitude sickness before can suddenly come down with it. Mountain sickness is rarely fatal but usually extremely uncomfortable. Victims complain of headaches, a sudden lack of coordination, shortness of breath, stomach upset, and a kind of drunken feeling. This occurs because the air at high altitudes contains less oxygen.

However, there are people who can live at high altitudes. They have adapted physiologically to their environment, thus, they have larger lungs and more blood in their system than people living at lower altitudes. Their hearts are also reportedly 20 percent larger!

The best cure for severe mountain sickness is to descend to a lower altitude. In mild cases, the victim should rest for three or four days to allow the circulatory system to adjust. In Peru, Bolivia, and Ecuador, the customary cure for *soroche* is an herbal tea made from coca leaves.

ISLANDS OF ADVENTURE

Easter Island and the Juan Fernández Islands in the South Pacific are Chile's islands of adventure. Both territories have interesting histories.

Easter Island is one of the world's most isolated islands and has an ancient and mysterious history. Acquired by Chile in 1888, Easter Island now has about 2,000 inhabitants. Some of them are Polynesian and call the island by its original name, Rapa Nui ("Large Island"). The island contains over 600 carved human-like figures called Moais that date as far back as

Mystery surrounds these stone statues called Moais. There are 600 of them on Easter Island.

A.D. 900. The figures have elongated heads, protruding eyebrows and chins, and small mouths. Many have distended ear lobes and carved ear ornaments. Some of the figures are only seven feet (2 m) high, while the tallest stands at a height of about 70 feet (21 m). As they are made of stone, even the smaller statues weigh many tons. The largest statue weighs over 280,000 pounds (140 tons).

How these large figures were carved and transported to sites around the island and why they were shaped as they were continues to be a mystery. Traditionally, it has been suggested that the statues are representations of sacred chiefs or important figures. Experts agree that the Moais were originally used as religious idols and later used to decorate and protect burial sites.

The major island in the Juan Fernández group is known as Robinson Crusoe Island. The real Crusoe, a Scottish sailor named Alexander Selkirk, was stranded on the island in 1704. Daniel Defoe modeled his hero after Selkirk, but set his novel thousands of miles away in the Caribbean.

After an argument with his captain, Selkirk defiantly asked to be left on the uninhabited island in the Juan Fernández group. As he disliked seafood, goats became his major source of nourishment. When rescued four years later, he could barely speak English and wore goat hides. He became quite a celebrity when he reached London but said, "I shall never be so happy as when I was not worth a farthing." He even tried to build a cave behind his father's house in Scotland just like the one he lived in on the island. He left for sea again in 1717 and died from a fever on board a ship in 1723.

Robinson Crusoe Island has little in common with the island described in Daniel Defoe's book. What the two islands have in common is the marooned hero who was cut off from society for several years.

CLIMATE

Chile is located in the Southern Hemisphere, so December and January are the warmest months, and July and August the coldest. Due to its stringbean length, Chile has many climatic regions.

The Atacama Desert in the north is one of the driest places on earth; in many parts, it rains only once a decade. The average annual temperature in Arica, near the Peruvian border, is a surprisingly cool 69°F (20.5°C) in January and 57°F (13.9°C) in July, due to the Humboldt Current, which moderates the temperature. Humidity is very high in the coastal areas, as rain falls along the coast and in the coastal range.

Santiago, in the Central Valley, has a stable, pleasant climate. Temperatures average 84°F (28.9°C) in summer and seldom go lower than 32°F (0°C) in winter. Average annual rainfall in the capital is 14 inches (35.6 cm), about the same as in Athens or Madrid. Mornings are often chilly, but never frigid, and afternoons are rarely so hot as to be oppressive.

As one moves south, temperatures drop and rainfall increases. In Valdivia, the average annual temperature is 53°F (11.7°C) and the average annual rainfall 98 inches (2.5 m). Strong winds blow year-round. In the southernmost town of Punta Arenas, the average annual temperature is 43°F (6.1°C). Some places have an average rainfall of 216 inches (548.6 cm) a year. There is little seasonal change in these regions. In some areas, the bad weather is so unrelenting that places have names like Hill of Anguish and Ice Water Valley.

Pink Chilean flamingos.

FLORA AND FAUNA

The Atacama Desert has almost no plant life due to the lack of rain. At high altitudes, certain species of cactus manage to survive by absorbing water from the fog called *camanchaca* ("kah-mahn-CHA-kah"), which occasionally blankets the peaks. The "candle holder" cactus, which is found at 6,000 feet (1,829 m), grows less than an inch (2.5 cm) a year.

Animal life in the Atacama is just as scarce, but in an area where temperatures surpass 120°F (48.9°C) during the day, a desert seagull called the gray gull is known to nest in the desert. When one parent gull flies to the coast to look for food, the other stands over their chick to shield the chick from the scorching sun. Gray gulls are said to pant like dogs during the hottest part of the day, before the afternoon breeze from the coast sweeps across the sand.

Guanacos, the small llamas of Chile.

Alpacas, vicuñas, llamas, and pink flamingos can be found at higher altitudes. Llamas, alpacas, and vicuñas are members of the camel family and have been prevalent in South America for two to three million years. Now, these animals have been domesticated and cannot live apart from humans, who keep them for their milk, meat, and coats. Wool from these animals can be made into handsome garments.

The rich soil of the Central Valley is perfect for cultivating cereal, fruit, and grapes. Common trees here include the palm, poplar, weeping willow, and eucalyptus. South of Concepción, almost half the land is covered by forest. Chile's national flower, the *copihue* of the lily family, grows in the wild in the Temuco area from October to July. The *araucaria* or monkey puzzle tree, an evergreen, grows south of the Bío-Bío River. Its high-quality wood is free of knots, making it the ideal substance for carving.

Birds such as the black-necked swan, wild goose, flamingo, penguin, and condor, whose wingspan can reach 17 feet (5.2 m), populate the southern regions of Patagonia and Magallanes. Pumas, red foxes, and small llamas called guanacos are plentiful in these regions.

The pudu or dwarf deer lives in the rain forests of southern Chile.

An almond orchard. The rich soil and mild climate of the Central Valley are ideal for growing cash crops.

Measuring only 15 inches (38 cm) tall and weighing less than 25 pounds (11 kg) when full-grown, the pudu is the world's smallest deer; a week-old baby pudu can sit comfortably in one hand. Pudus resemble tiny antelopes with fox-like faces and spotted coats. They are solitary and travel alone. All day and night, they dart in and out of the dense forest undergrowth while snacking on leaves and berries and taking short rests. At one time, pudus were common in parts of the Chilean and Argentine Andes. Now, their numbers are scarce and they are an endangered species in the region.

Some 200 species of fish from the Pacific Ocean can be found along Chile's western coast. From the northern coast come tuna, swordfish, sole, smelt, sardine, red and black conger eel, which are a national culinary specialty, octopus, clam, crab, mussel, and abalone. Lobster and shrimp can be found off the central coast, while salmon and trout can be found in rivers and lakes.

HISTORY

RECENT DISCOVERIES AT MONTE VERDE suggest that parts of Chile were inhabited as early as 14,500 years ago. Some 3,500 years later, the Atacameños arrived in the area north of the Atacama Salt Flat. They lived as hunter-gatherers until about 1500 B.C., when they began to farm and set up permanent villages.

Archaeologists have also studied the Chinchorro culture, which existed in Chile between 8000 and 1000 B.C. Many mummies and tools of the Chinchorro have been dug up in sites near Arica, some of which are more than 7,800 years old. Studies done on these mummies reveal that many of the Chichorro men probably went deaf from diving for shellfish, while the women had an unusual arthritis of the neck from carrying heavy loads. A high-protein diet gave the Chinchorro strong teeth. Tools found, such as nets and harpoons, indicate that the Chinchorro were expert fishermen.

The Atacameño group has left numerous geoglyphs sprawled across the Atacama Desert over an area of over 100 square miles (259 square km). These geoglyphs depict animals such as llamas, lizards, cats, birds, and fish. The smallest drawing is about 3.3 feet (1 m) tall and the largest, the Atacama Giant, is about 380 feet (115 m) in height. These mysterious images were drawn along an old Andean trade route. Thousand-year-old mummies of the Atacameño culture have also been found.

In 1954, gold miners stumbled across the perfectly preserved 500-year-old body of an Incan boy in the Chilean Andes. Scientists believe he was of noble birth and was sacrificed to the sun god during a festival.

Opposite: **A mummy displayed in the Museo Atacama in Chile.**

Below: **Some geoglyphs are more than 150 feet (46 m) high and depict people, dogs, eagles, condors, and vicuñas.**

SPANISH CONQUEST

In the early 1400s, the Incas from Peru came across Chile's northern desert and took the northern half of what is now the Central Valley. Their attempts to claim more territory in the south were foiled by the Araucanians, also

Statue of a Mapuche leader.

called Mapuche Indians, who resisted the invaders with great ferocity. In the mid-16th century, at the time of the Spanish conquest, the country had some one million Indians from several different groups.

The Portuguese explorer Fernando de Magallanes— or Ferdinand Magellan, as he is called in English—sailed through what is now called the Strait of Magellan in 1520. He was the first European to see the southern region called Tierra del Fuego. In about 1535, Spanish conquistador Diego de Almagro came to Chile from Peru in search of gold and silver. He got as far as what is now Santiago before turning back. The town of Santiago was officially founded by Spaniard Pedro de Valdivia in 1541.

The Mapuche were one of the few groups in the New World to win repeated battles against the Spanish. Valdivia himself was murdered by the Mapuche in 1554. They were clever warriors who stole Spanish horses and used them to raid Spanish towns. Eventually, the Mapuche men gave up farm life and devoted themselves to warfare.

Despite their success in war, the Mapuche were not as sophisticated as the Incas. They did not build cities and had few advanced tools. They lived in simple one-room huts made from wooden poles, straw, and animal skins. Their language was complex, however, and they loved sports, especially a game called *chueca* ("CHWAY-kah"), which resembles field hockey. In the mid-17th century, the Indians signed a peace treaty with the

"...this land is such that there is none better in the world."

—*Valdivia, writing about Chile, in a letter to the Spanish king.*

20

Spanish, but the Mapuche were not really stopped until the late 1800s.

Before he died, Valdivia divided much of the agricultural land in Chile among his soldiers and gave them Indian slaves to farm the land in a system called the *encomienda* ("ehn-KOH-mee-EHN-dah"). When slavery was outlawed, Indians became tenant farmers, or *inquilinos* ("een-kee-LEE-nos"), on large plantations, or *haciendas* ("ah-see-EHN-dahs").

Each *hacienda* or *fundo* ("FOON-doh") was a society in itself. It had its own store, church, and sometimes school. Indians lived in huts on the estate, kept some livestock, and had small patches of land to grow food for themselves. Ideally, for the Spanish, the Indians were devoted to the landowners. To cement their loyalty, the landowners participated in rodeos and festivals with the Indians. The *fundo* system persisted in Chile until the mid-20th century.

During the colonial period, Chile was run by a governor who answered to the viceroyalty of Peru in Lima. The Spanish authority forbade Chile to trade with the other Spanish colonies, and this led to smuggling. Due to many such restrictions placed on the Chileans, many of the landowners gradually lost their loyalty to Spain, which had little interest in a land with scarce gold resources and an indomitable group of Indians.

Pedro de Valdivia, the Spanish explorer who founded the city of Santiago, now the capital of Chile.

THE INDEPENDENCE MOVEMENT

In the early 19th century, Spain controlled territory stretching from California in the north to Cape Horn in the south, from the Pacific Ocean in the west to the mouth of Venezuela's Orinoco River in the east. Less than 20 years later, the only Spanish colonies left were Cuba and Puerto Rico.

The disappearance of Spanish colonies was due to independence movements emerging all over Latin America. These movements came about for several reasons. The Spanish held their colonies back from economic prosperity by imposing strict trade laws. Spanish born in the New World considered themselves more South American than Spanish and drew inspiration from the American and French independence movements in the late 1700s.

On September 18, 1810, the first autonomous government was declared. Spain later reclaimed Chile. It was not until Argentine-born José de San Martín and his army made their way into Chile from Argentina in 1817 that the final victory came into view. Claiming that he "came to liberate Chile, not to rule it," San Martín appointed a member of his army, Bernardo O'Higgins, the son of an Irish

A Spanish fort built in 1645.

immigrant, as head of the new government. Independence was officially proclaimed on February 12, 1818, but it is celebrated on September 18 every year.

O'Higgins, the father of Chile's independence, was an intellectual interested in making cultural, economic, and educational progress in Chile, even among the poor. He built schools, a library, and lighting and sanitation systems in Santiago. However, wealthy landowners, who continued to influence Chilean politics and society, and the leaders of the Catholic Church did not approve of O'Higgins. He was ousted in 1823 and sent into exile in Peru, where he died without ever seeing Chile again.

Civil war began in 1830, and the landowners won. In 1833, they adopted a constitution that benefited themselves and the powerful president they elected.

THE 19TH CENTURY

By the 19th century, Chile had won the War of the Pacific (1879–83) against Peru and Bolivia. The victory expanded the country's territory by a third and gave it possession of the Atacama Desert, which had rich deposits of nitrate, a natural fertilizer. Exportation of nitrate gave Chile an important source of income for 40 years, and the mining industry created jobs for a new group that soon became the middle class.

The statue of Arturo Alessandri Palma, in front of La Moneda, the presidential palace, in the Plaza de la Libertad.

President José Manuel Balmaceda, who took office in 1886, was the first leader to attempt to place some of the country's wealth in the hands of the middle class. The upper class and the British, Chile's important trading partner, disliked Balmaceda's policies for social reform, and he was deposed in 1891. Again, civil war ensued and 10,000 Chileans lost their lives.

MODERN CHILE

In 1920, Arturo Alessandri Palma was elected by the working and middle classes in another attempt to reduce the power of landowners and narrow the gap between rich and poor. Alessandri was ousted by a military takeover in 1924 but returned to power in 1925. He wrote a new constitution that separated Church from State, authorized tax reforms, and ensured freedom of worship and new laws to help the poor. Literate males over 21 were given the right to vote (women's suffrage did not come about until 1940.) The 1925 constitution governed politics in Chile until 1973.

The 1930s were marked by the Great Depression and the fall of nitrate prices after the invention of artificial nitrates. Many political parties were created in this period. Despite the turmoil, Chile was considered the most invulnerable democracy in South America. Elections were held regularly and the press had great freedom.

In 1964, Eduardo Frei was elected to the presidency, the first Christian Democratic candidate to ever win a presidential election in Latin America. Frei began far-reaching social programs for the poor in housing, education, and land redistribution. During his time in office, unemployment and inflation rose.

In 1970, Salvador Allende Gossens, a Marxist and member of the Socialist Party, was elected president by a narrow margin. He took over many of Chile's privately-owned industries and banks and redistributed land owned by the upper class. Allende never had the support of the Chilean congress, and he could not gather the support of most Chileans. During his last years in power, the economy faltered and inflation soared. In 1973, the inflation rate was more than 300 percent. There were mass demonstrations, strikes, and widespread rural unrest due to shortages of food and consumer goods.

On September 11, 1973, the military, consisting of the army, air force, navy, and national police, overthrew the Allende government in a violent coup d'état. The presidential palace was attacked, and the president and his supporters fought back. During the coup, Allende died, apparently having committed suicide. Although Allende's term was short, he left a permanent legacy in Chile for his sincere attempts at social reform.

President and social reformist from 1970 to 1973, Salvador Allende Gossens.

GOVERNMENT

UNTIL THE EARLY 1970s, Chile was thought to be one of the most stable democratic nations in South America. But in 1973, the government of Salvador Allende Gossens, who was elected president in 1970, was overthrown by the armed forces. The military government that replaced him was led by General Augusto Pinochet Ugarte.

Opposite: **The courts of justice in Santiago.**

Allende's government had placed a lot of emphasis on social programs, and the Chilean economy had suffered greatly during its administration. Pinochet vowed to purge the country of Marxists and revitalize the economy. His military dictatorship would shape the country's political and social reality for the next 17 years.

Immediately following the coup in 1973, Chile was ruled by a junta, or a small group of leaders, consisting of the commanders-in-chief of the four military forces. Eventually, General Pinochet, the commander of the army, emerged as the chief executive. He chose his cabinet, and his government appointed regional administrators, provincial governors, mayors of the cities, and rectors of the state universities.

In 1988, Pinochet allowed Chileans to decide whether he should remain their chief executive for another eight years. Fifty-five percent voted in favor of a presidential election and an election was held in 1989. The Pinochet government lost the election and had to step down from power. Thousands of Chileans thronged the streets of Santiago to celebrate the end of the dictatorship.

Chileans elected Patricio Aylwin, the leader of the Christian Democratic Party, president. During his presidency, Aylwin was considered a moderate, the person who would lead Chile in its transition to democracy. When he took office, he stated that his priorities would be to convict those responsible for human rights crimes, maintain economic stability, and narrow the gap between rich and poor.

Women demonstrate for the "disappeared."

THE "DISAPPEARED"

From 1973 to 1989, those opposing Pinochet were sent to prisoner camps, where they were tortured or killed. Some 10,000 Chileans were banished; many others were arrested and detained. Congress was terminated, the constitution suspended, press freedoms curbed, political parties banned, and other institutions heavily controlled. The national police swarmed the streets in Santiago, and protesters were attacked by trained dogs, fired upon with water cannons, or arrested. At times, rigid curfews were set, and those who did not keep to the hours were rounded up by the national police. Books critical of the government were banned or burned, and their authors punished. When, or if, elections were held, they were often rigged. Men were taken away in the middle of the night, and their wives' pleas for information on their whereabouts were ignored. The missing people came to be known as the "disappeared."

Rally for Aylwin's party.

RETURN TO DEMOCRACY

In the 1989 presidential elections, Chileans had to choose between a former Pinochet minister and a Christian Democrat, Patricio Aylwin, who represented the Concertación ("con-sehr-tah-see-OHN"), a union of center- and left-wing democratic political parties. Aylwin won and took over the presidency in 1990. He vowed to reinstate press and political freedoms, release political prisoners, and allow exiles to return. At the same time, his government chose to continue many of the economic programs implemented by the Pinochet government.

Elections were held again in 1993, and Eduardo Frei, the Concertación candidate, took office in 1994. Then in 1999, Ricardo Lagos, also representing the Concertación, became the first Socialist to be elected president since Allende. His government has continued the policies of the two previous governments.

THE PINOCHET CASE

After stepping down from the presidency in 1989, Pinochet was named a senator-for-life in the Chilean National Congress.

In 1998, he flew to London for medical treatment and was arrested for human rights abuses committed during his 17-year rule. Ironically, it was not a Chilean, but a Spanish judge who ordered his arrest and extradition. The British government put him under house arrest, while the legal system decided if he could be extradited to Spain. After more than a year, the British courts decided that Pinochet was too ill and allowed him to return to Chile.

Pinochet supporters, who made up over 30 percent of the population, came out to welcome him home, while families of the disappeared protested and called for his arrest. Despite the warm welcome by his supporters, Pinochet returned to a different Chile. In June 2000, he was stripped of immunity against prosecution granted by his position as senator-for-life. In July 2001, 85-year-old Pinochet was saved by his ailing health as the appeals court in Santiago ruled that he was unfit to stand trial.

Pinochet has been named in over 250 human rights cases in Chile. His case is significant not only for Chile, but is also a message to other dictators that they can no longer commit crimes against people without expecting a backlash from the international community.

THE LEGISLATURE

Chile is a republic. It is headed by a chief executive, the president, who is elected for a six-year, non-renewable term. The president lives in his own home in Santiago. The executive offices are in La Moneda, the presidential palace. The president appoints cabinet ministers.

The seat of the legislative branch of the government was moved to the city of Valparaíso by the Pinochet government. The legislature is made up of two houses: the Senate and the Chamber of Deputies. Senators are elected for eight-year terms, and deputies for four-year terms. In 2001, there were 120 deputies, 38 senators, and nine senators-for-life.

THE JUDICIARY

The Supreme Court is the high court of the judicial branch of the government. Supreme Court judges are appointed for life by the chief executive. Chile's 11 courts of appeal consist of judges appointed by the president from a list made up by Supreme Court judges. Similarly, judges of lower courts are chosen by the president from a list compiled by judges of the courts of appeal. During Pinochet's rule, a separate military tribunal was organized to try opponents of the regime. This tribunal has since been abolished.

REGIONAL ADMINISTRATION

There are 13 regions in Chile administered by "intendants" appointed by the president. These regions are divided into provinces administered by governors. The provinces are further divided into municipalities administered by mayors, who are directly elected by the people.

During the Pinochet years, his supporters pervaded positions of power at every level.

La Moneda, the presidential palace in Santiago, was originally built as a mint. This is the source of its name, which means "the coin."

ECONOMY

CHILE HAS ONE OF THE HEALTHIEST economies in South America. Inflation is low, and the country has the highest savings rate in all of Latin America. However, Chile was strongly affected by the Asian economic crisis in 1998, and in the first three months of 2001, unemployment rose to 8.8 percent due to a worldwide economic slowdown.

Much of Chile's success can be attributed to extensive exportation of local goods. Chile exports over 3,800 products to over 172 countries. Between 1989 and 1999, exports grew by an annual average of 9.5 percent. The United States is Chile's primary trading partner, especially in fruit exports. Because Chile is located south of the equator, it can put summer fruits like grapes and berries on North American tables in winter.

The new wealth created during Pinochet's rule went mostly into the hands of those who were already well-off. When Pinochet left the government, one-third of all Chileans were living in poverty. Under the democratic governments, this proportion has dropped to less than a quarter. Today, practically every Chilean has access to water and electricity. Although government housing programs have eradicated most shantytowns, about 5 percent of the population is considered indigent, or extremely poor. Many people have had to create their own jobs to survive. This is known as the informal market. Chileans who are not formerly employed peddle cheap goods in the streets, clean car windshields, search the city for used newspapers to sell to recycling centers, or beg for money.

Although the number of poor in Chile is high, the situation is better than in other Latin American countries. Most Chileans have seen an increase in their standard of living. They own television sets, cars, their own homes, and many have joined private pension and health care plans, which are quite rare in Latin America. The government tries to maintain the high growth rate, while introducing social programs to aid the poor.

Opposite: **Workers pack fish into cans at a factory at Chiloe. Fishing is one of Chile's major industries.**

TWO LITTLE GRAPES

The Chilean grape export business made international headlines in March 1989 when cyanide was found in grapes shipped to the United States. The food scare began when the U.S. Food and Drug Administration (FDA) received telephone threats that Chilean grape shipments had been poisoned with cyanide. Suddenly, the entire fruit export business came to a halt: shipments were impounded in all U.S., Canadian, Japanese, and West German ports, and over 100,000 Chilean fruit workers lost their jobs. In the end, officials found harmless amounts of cyanide in just two red grapes.

Although most North Americans soon forgot the incident, many Chileans still have not recovered from the damage the scare caused the grape industry. Angry Chilean politicians, farmers, and exporters claim that the U.S. government should pay some US$333 million in damages to compensate for the losses incurred.

"The damage is much more than US$333 million," said Chilean Senator Sergio Romero, "because this involves the dignity of a country and the prestige of the fruit, on which you cannot put a price."

EXPORTS AND FOREIGN INVESTMENTS

In 2000, the per capita income in Chile was approximately US$4,700. The gross domestic product (GDP) in the same year totaled US$70.2 billion. The agricultural sector made up about 8.4 percent of the GDP. Major agricultural products included wheat, potatoes, corn, sugar beets, onions, beans, fresh vegetables, fresh fruit, and livestock. The industrial and manufacturing sector accounted for 34.2 percent of the GDP. The main industrial activities were concentrated in textiles, metal manufacturing, food processing, pulp, paper, and wood products.

Chile's exports in 2000 were worth around US$18 billion. Major export products included copper, fruit, fish meal, and cellulose. The country's main trading partners are the United States, Japan, Argentina, and Brazil.

An industrial workshop in Santiago.

The European Union (EU) is Chile's largest export market. Imports in 2000 totaled over US$16 billion. The main imports included industrial equipment, petroleum, chemical products, and consumer goods.

Chile enjoys a high level of foreign investment. The United States is the biggest investor. Most investments are made in the mining sector, but communications, construction, forestry, and fishing also benefit.

MINING

Minerals are a significant source of revenue for Chile. Mining accounts for about 40 percent of total exports. Copper is Chile's single most important source of wealth, accounting for most of the country's export earnings. Chile has about 20 percent of the world's copper reserves and has been the world's largest producer of copper since 1982. The most important mine, Chuquicamata, is 2 miles (3.2 km) long, half a mile (800 m) wide, and 1,000 feet (305 m) deep.

Chile also produces other minerals such as molybdenum, iron ore, manganese, sulfur, and nitrates, once a major source of revenue. The Atacama Desert has the world's largest natural nitrate deposit and is home to 58 percent of the world's lithium reserves. Chile possesses 14 percent of the world's supply of iodine and jumped from the 36th position to being the second largest iodine producer in the world.

Chile has limited reserves of crude oil and imports 95 percent of its petroleum supply. Coal was mined heavily in the past, but major mines near Concepción have been closed down.

Opposite: **Sulfur ore in the Atacama Desert. In the background is Volcán Tocopuri.**

Below: **Processing wood for manufacture in the Lake District in Chile.**

MANUFACTURING AND INDUSTRY

The manufacturing and industry sector accounts for about one-third of the GDP and employs 27 percent of the workforce. Products from this sector include wine and beverages, wood products, food products, metal products, textiles, plastics, chemicals, and leather and shoes. These are primarily exported to the United States, other Latin American countries, and Japan. More than 80 percent of manufacturing jobs are in the cities of Santiago, Valparaíso, and Concepción.

A fish-packing factory.

AGRICULTURE

Most of the farming in Chile takes place in the fertile 600-mile-long (966-km-long) Central Valley. Despite the economic crisis in 2001, the agricultural sector continued to grow, led by the production of avocados, apples, kiwis, and cherries. Livestock production is limited to beef, poultry, and pork. Sheep are raised on farms in the southern regions of the country.

The agricultural industry employs about 14 percent of the workforce. Many Chilean farm workers are nomadic; they move from farm to farm, harvesting whatever crops are in season.

FORESTRY AND FISHING

Chile is one of the world's top fishing nations. Traditional fishing accounts for about 60 percent of production. Most fishing is done off the northern coast, where the main product is fishmeal, used as animal feed. The other 40 percent of the fish supply is raised on fish farms in the south. Chile

exports a lot of fish and is the world's second largest producer of salmon.

Chile has more than a million acres (4,047 square km) of pine tree plantations. Most of them are located in the south, where the climate is more conducive to the growth of this evergreen. Most of the pine lumber is used to make pulp and paper products.

A young farmer with his harvest of potatoes.

CHILE'S WINE INDUSTRY

The fertile lands located three hours south of Santiago are one of the most exciting wine regions in the world. Stretching from Aconcagua Province through Colchagua Province and south to the towns of Sagrada Familia, Lontué, and Molina, this wine country has ideal climate, irrigation, and soil quality, and no harmful insects.

Vines were originally planted in Chile in the 1500s to make wine for the Eucharist in the Catholic Mass. In the mid-1850s, a Chilean wine-grower employed a French wine specialist to grow grapes that would make fine wines. In the 1860s, a blight struck the European vineyards, wiping out most of the crops for many years. The only top quality vineyards that remained untouched were those in Chile. By 1889, Chilean wines were winning important prizes in Paris.

Today, Chile is the largest exporter of wines in Latin America. It exports to more than 50 countries, including Japan, the United States, Canada, Great Britain, Colombia, Venezuela, Argentina, and Brazil. Wine has steadily increased in importance in the Chilean economy, supplying both export revenue and jobs; wine exports grew dramatically from US$13 million in 1986 to US$501 million in 1998.

Chilean winemakers use European methods. They ferment the grapes in vats. White wine is aged one- to one-and-a-half years, while red wine is bottled after two- to two-and-a-half years. Most Chileans drink cheap varieties sold in grocery stores as *tinto* ("TEEN-toh"), or red, and *blanco* ("BLAHN-koh"), or white. Experts have noted that Chilean wines are great bargains in both quality and price.

THE CHILEAN WORK DAY

Like in the United States, the typical Chilean work day starts at 9 A.M. and ends at 6 P.M., although businesspeople often work until 7 or 8 P.M. Chileans are among the few Latin Americans who do not take long lunch hours followed by siestas, or naps. Shops downtown are usually open only half a day on Saturday. Everything is closed on Sunday, except the new megamalls, which stay open until 10 P.M., seven days a week.

At the stock market in Santiago.

Chilean businesspeople are generally conservative. They dislike aggression and are known to be very trustworthy and honorable when making deals. Women are taken seriously in the workforce and need not be overly aggressive to have their opinions heard. Decisions are often made by only the top management.

Chileans like an introductory session where they get to know their customer before discussing business. Typical topics of conversation include family, leisure activities like fishing or skiing, and Chilean wines.

ENVIRONMENT

CHILE IS RICH IN NATURAL RESOURCES and derives much of its wealth from the land. The northern region, characterized by the rugged beauty of the desert, has vast mineral deposits. The Central Valley is a source of fruit, vegetables, and wine. The southern region, lush with forests, lakes, and volcanoes, earns its livelihood from the forestry, dairy, and paper industries. The long coastline harbors fish and shellfish.

The Chilean economy depends heavily on its natural resources, but as a developing country, Chile has not always had enough money to devote to environmental causes. As a result, pollution has reached dangerous levels, biodiversity has decreased, and marine resources have dwindled. Only in the 1990s did a democratic government begin to take major steps to prevent further harm to the environment. Eighteen percent of Chilean territory has been turned into national parks. Progress has been slow, but Chileans are starting to demand results.

A study of environmental issues conducted in the early 1990s showed that many government bodies were implementing divergent or overlapping environmental policies. In 1994, the government created the National Commission on the Environment (CONAMA) to oversee a coordinated national environmental policy and to work with industry and the public.

Above: **An odd-shaped cactus flourishes in the harsh climate of the desert.**

Opposite: **The Salto de Laja waterfall is a site of natural grandeur.**

Wildlife and scenic beauty lie side by side at the Lauca national park.

BIOLOGICAL DIVERSITY

Chile is home to at least 29,000 different animal species. Biological diversity in Chile has declined, but because there has been no consistent detailed investigation, it is not known which species have been most affected. Different regions have been studied using various methods, and some ecosystems have never been studied at all. Nevertheless, conservation efforts are underway. As part of the Convention on Biodiversity, an international convention of which Chile became a party in 1994, CONAMA has implemented the National System of Information on Biodiversity in Chile. Studies carried out as part of this project will provide relevant organizations with the data needed to protect Chile's biological diversity.

The areas most affected are the Central Valley, the coastal mountain range, and the Andes pre-range. Human activities such as the building of dams, the random introduction of new species, and overhunting, as well as soil erosion and pollution, are responsible for habitat destruction. The southern river otter and short-tailed chinchilla are endangered animals. The vicuña, a relative of the llama, was on the verge of extinction, but thanks to a government policy, there are now over 20,000 vicuñas in Chile.

The Toromiro tree from Easter Island is now extinct in the wild. Some trees still exist in a handful of botanical gardens around the world, but they are unable to reproduce on their own. The conservation of the tree is carried out in a laboratory.

PRECIOUS MARINE RESOURCES

Just about every Chilean has access to drinking water. However, there are problems with the disposal of waste water from homes, factories, mines, and agricultural areas, which have high levels of pesticides. Sewage systems are very expensive, so for many years, waste was dumped directly into rivers and the Pacific Ocean. Almost all of the country's water treatment plants were built during the 1990s. The government has privatized sanitation systems, reducing the amount of untreated domestic waste. Yet, as the population continues to grow, there is more waste and an increased demand for drinking water. In the late 1990s, laws were introduced to regulate industrial waste disposal. As of 2001, these laws have not yet been passed. Once these laws are passed, however, it is expected that at least 70 percent of all industrial waste will be controlled. Small industries that require technical assistance will be exempt.

The fishing industry is a key part of the Chilean economy. Chile exports many types of fish and exotic seafood, and it is the world's largest supplier of fishmeal. However, many species have been over-harvested, and fish populations have dropped. During the 1990s, there was a noticeable fall in the size of fish catches, especially in the case of jurel, or southern jack mackerel, which fell by 60 percent in 1998. The number of *locos*, a type of abalone, dropped to such critical levels that it became illegal to harvest or sell them. They have, however, made a comeback and can once again be harvested, although within strict limits. Fishing laws have been criticized for their inability to effectively protect Chile's marine species.

Salmon is one of Chile's main exports. Salmon are raised on fish farms, and this prevents over-fishing. However, fish farms are known to contaminate the surroundings with antibiotics and waste. Conservationists complain that laws governing fish farms are not strict enough.

The Bío-Bío River, famous among white water rafters for its rapids, has been dammed to provide hydroelectric power, which meets most of Chile's energy needs.

LAND USE

Only a small proportion of Chilean land is suitable for agriculture. Chile has suffered from land erosion for more than 100 years due to animal grazing, poor farming techniques, and urbanization. The government has initiated programs to stop desertification, but unless land is used with long-term goals in mind instead of short-term needs, these efforts will be in vain.

Another problem is the overuse of pesticides in agriculture. It has been difficult to study their effects on the environment because it is not known which pesticides are used, where, and in what quantities. The only information available is how much of a certain pesticide has been imported into the country. The Agriculture and Animal Husbandry Service (SAG) under the Ministry of Agriculture, is responsible for constantly reviewing pesticides in use.

In Chile, garbage is disposed of in dumps, many of which are illegal and almost full. Furthermore, Chile does not have an official recycling program. Glass, paper, and aluminum products can be sold for recycling purposes. These are often collected by *cartoneros* ("kahr-toh-NEH-rohs"), people who scour the streets at night for paper or cardboard to sell for money.

A substantial percentage of arable land in Chile is devoted to orchards as fruit export provides important income for the economy.

SAVING THE FORESTS

Chile is blessed with abundant forests, primarily in the south. However, these forests are slowly being replaced by tree plantations. In fact, the Maule and Bío-Bío regions already have more plantations than forests. Areas are cleared of natural vegetation, and then the seeds of the radiata pine tree are sown; this tree grows far more quickly in Chile than in other parts of the world. The logged trees are used to make pulp, cellulose, paper products, and furniture. The whole venture may be a success economically, but it causes soil erosion and the loss of habitat for various species of plants and animals.

The reason for the environment crisis in Chile is that there was practically no regulation of forestry during the Pinochet era. Laws were only passed by the democratic government during the 1990s to protect indigenous forests, but Chile still lacks a clear national policy on the issue. There are conflicting ideas on how to manage forest resources. The National Forest Corporation (CONAF) oversees the Working Group for Managing a Sustainable Forest, a body made up of conservationists, industrialists, academics, and government officials. The goal of this group is to build agreements on how to best use Chile's forests.

Extensive logging in Chile has cost the country many of its lush natural forests.

SAVING THE AIR

The most obvious environmental problem in Chile is air pollution, particularly in Santiago. The capital lies in a valley, and a phenomenon called thermal inversion, affecting the circulation of wind, traps polluted air in the valley. As a result, a huge brown cloud covers the city, especially in winter. When the rains come, the air is cleaned, and the skies are blue. But after a few days, the pollution returns. Smog is the cause of many health problems, primarily respiratory illnesses.

Most of the pollution is caused by human activities. The biggest sources of pollution are vehicle and factory emissions, dust, and forest fires. The government has implemented a number of measures to help correct the situation. First, a law was passed requiring each new car purchased to be equipped with a catalytic converter to help reduce emissions. There is also a program called Restricción ("rehs-treek-see-OHN"), which restricts cars without catalytic converters from driving one day a week between March and December. Each month, a new schedule is made, and the day of restriction is based on the last number of the license plate.

Now, the government is deciding whether to also restrict cars with catalytic converters. Even though Restricción helps reduce pollution, it cannot keep the number of vehicles from rising. Between 1990 and 1998, the number of vehicles on the street almost doubled.

To help cut factory emissions, no new industries are allowed to set up operations in the Santiago metropolitan area. Some industries have also been forced to shut down part or all of their operations. Because this can be quite expensive, many factories have moved away from Santiago.

Paving all the streets in Santiago would help to reduce dust and pollution in the city. Average temperatures, however, would rise.

Despite strict regulations, traffic congestion is still a big problem in Santiago.

CHILEANS

MORE THAN 15 MILLION PEOPLE make up the Chilean population. The largest ethnic group consists of *mestizos* ("mehs-TEE-sos"), or people of mixed Spanish and Indian blood. The second largest group is European, and the smallest group is indigenous Indian, mostly Mapuche. There are also the Polynesians of Easter Island and small groups of Arabs and Asians.

Even though most Chileans have some Indian blood, they are sensitive about the subject of mixed ethnicity. In general, Chileans see themselves as Caucasians and are far more greatly influenced by European and North American cultures than by early Indian culture.

Chileans are not as ethnically diverse as other Latin Americans. In fact, Chile is said to be one of the most homogeneous countries in South America. Immigrants did not settle in Chile in great numbers the way they did in Brazil and Argentina, and Chile's unique, protected geography has kept it rather isolated from the rest of the world.

However, small groups of German, French, Italian, and Swiss immigrants did come to Chile in the mid-1800s. People from England, Ireland, Croatia, Palestine, and Korea immigrated in later years. Some typical non-Spanish Chilean surnames are Edwards, Lyon, Schmidt, Newman, and Ross.

Central Chile has only 18 percent of the nation's land, but about 80 percent of its people. Today, more than 85 percent of Chileans live in urban areas, compared to only 68 percent in 1960 and 20 percent a hundred years ago. Of the urban population, 40 percent reside in Santiago, the

Opposite and below: **Despite the tremendous length of the country, Chileans enjoy a homogenous culture.**

capital. Other populous cities are Valparaíso-Viña del Mar, Concepción, and Temuco, all in central Chile, and Antofagasta near the Atacama Desert. Many German immigrants settled in the southern cities of Valdivia, Llanquihue, and Osorno. Most Croatians have made their home in Tierra del Fuego in the south, and the Mapuche Indians live mainly in the southern Central Valley near the city of Temuco. The Aymara live in the far north near the borders of Bolivia and Peru, and the Rapa Nui live on Easter Island.

The fertility rate in Chile is 17.2 births per 1,000 people and population growth averages 1.3 percent per year.

The infant mortality rate is comparatively low. About 10 out of every 1,000 children die before their first birthday. The average life expectancy is 75.7 years. The major causes of death are heart disease and cancer.

Population Distribution in Chile:

Persons per square mile

nearly uninhabited

under 3

3–25

25–50

over 50

MESTIZOS

Mestizos make up the fundamental ethnic group in Chile. When Valdivia came to Chile, he brought only one Spanish woman, his mistress. His troops married indigenous Indian women. Within 50 years, the *mestizo* population had overtaken the European population. In colonial times, *mestizos* could be found at all levels of society; the same is true today, although they also make up a majority of the working class.

THE IMMIGRANTS

After the first Spanish colonists, the Basques from the Pyrenees were the next to immigrate to Chile in significant numbers. Arriving in the late 18th and early 19th centuries, they soon took jobs as merchants and traders and bought up large pieces of land. After two or three generations, they were firmly ensconced in the upper class. English, Irish, and Scottish immigrants followed the Basques.

In the mid-1800s, thousands of Germans migrated to Chile as part of a program to populate the country south of the Bío-Bío River. They found the climate similar to that of their German homeland and so set up homes and became farmers. Now, many Germans in Chile raise cattle for milk and grow crops such as potatoes, beets, and oats. Hotels and pastry shops with German names are common in this area of the country.

Descendants of Chile's immigrant population drive a herd of cattle down a country road that winds through the fertile Central Valley.

During the height of European immigration, between 1883 and 1901, only 36,000 Europeans came to Chile. (More migrated to the United States in a single month during the same period.) Although their numbers were small, the immigrants made a significant impact on Chilean society. They had been members of the educated middle class in their home countries and brought much-needed job skills to their new home.

Some 25,000 Slavs migrated to Chile in the late 19th century to take advantage of the gold rush in Tierra del Fuego. From there, many became successful fishermen, merchants, and shipbuilders. Today, many Chilean Slavs are professionals, government servants, and businessmen.

In the 20th century, the most significant immigrants were Palestinian. Most of them established small businesses, especially in textile manufacturing, that later became quite successful. Jews who came from Europe and the Middle East moved to the urban areas and started retail businesses. Koreans made up the latest wave of immigrants.

During Pinochet's rule, as many as one million Chileans, mostly professionals, intellectuals, and artists, were exiled to other Latin American countries, the United States, and Europe. In Pinochet's later years, he allowed many exiles to return. With the return of democracy, many Chileans have decided to come back to their homeland.

Women serve in the Chilean Air Force.

An Aymara Indian at a religious festival in northern Chile.

THE INDIANS

The Chilean Indian population was never particularly large or concentrated in any one area. The Atacameño and Diaguita peoples lived in the Atacama region; the Mapuche in the Central Valley and on Chiloé Island; and the Ona and Yagan peoples in the far south. None of these groups thrived in the presence of Europeans, as the Spanish conquest brought with it slavery, war, and fatal diseases like smallpox.

Only a small Chilean Indian population remains today. Groups such as the Ona, Yagan, and Diaguita have been completely wiped out. The largest Indian group in Chile, the Mapuche, stands at only about 400,000. The Mapuche fought the European settlers well into the late 19th century. They were the only Indians in North and South America to effectively resist the Spanish during the entire colonial period. It is said that the Mapuche never really surrendered; they simply stopped fighting.

Valdivia described the Mapuche as strong, handsome, friendly people who were fair in color. Other colonists wrote of their serious manner, their ability to withstand severe hardship, and their intimacy with the land they farmed. They did not build temples for they had no organized religion; they believed in magic and omens sent by trees, birds, or the wind. The women were said to be very beautiful in their bright-colored clothes, beaded jewelry, and headdresses. The men were fierce warriors.

Mapuche means "people of the land" and members of the group feel very strongly about the loss of their territory. They separate themselves from outsiders, whom they call *huincas* ("oo-EEN-kahs"), the wealthy landowners who do not look after their own people in times of need.

The Mapuche are a tight-knit community. They speak Spanish when they have to, but they have their own language. They feel that the government has treated them unfairly in giving them inadequate portions of land to farm. Generally, they are impoverished and have inadequate medical care and few opportunities for advancement. The Mapuche have consistently higher poverty and infant mortality rates and lower life expectancies than

A painting of Mapuche Indians armed with bolas carrying off women during a raid on the Spanish colonists.

the rest of the population. Infant mortality among the Mapuche is 34 per 1,000 births, compared with 10 per 1,000 for the entire Chilean population. Most Mapuche live south of the Bío-Bío River, but due to economic hardship, some have migrated to large cities like Santiago and Concepción.

CLASS STRUCTURE

The class structure of Chilean society resembles a pyramid: the small elite upper class is at the top, the growing middle class is in the center, and the massive lower class is at the bottom. The three classes have vastly different values, ways of life, and income levels.

THE ELITE UPPER CLASS This class includes the descendants of the Spanish colonists and the European migrants who came to Chile in the 19th and early 20th centuries. The children of English, Italian, Irish, and French immigrants have, for the most part, lost their languages and become wholly Chilean.

University students in Valdivia, a town in southern Chile with strong German influence.

The elite holds most of the country's wealth. In colonial times, the upper class family traditionally had a house in Santiago, land just outside the city, and a large country estate or *hacienda*. In the post-colonial era, the *hacienda* was often leased to a farmer who paid rent and kept the house for the owner's vacation use. Having a country estate is still a status symbol among the upper class.

Membership in Chile's upper class is open to foreigners who are sufficiently wealthy and educated. A wealthy immigrant could climb the social ladder by marrying into a good Chilean family and buying land. The children from this marriage would buy a trading house, a mine, or more land and marry into the elite class. By then, the third generation would be accepted into the elite and would then add to the family wealth by taking a position in the government. At this point, the family would have financial, social, and political power in the community. There is social mobility, and with the surge in the economy, a nouveau riche sector has emerged.

THE MIDDLE CLASS A hundred years ago, the middle class was made up of only a small group of merchants and small-scale businessmen. The discovery of nitrate and then copper provided significant employment opportunities for Chileans and started the country's modern labor force. Today, the middle class makes up the heart of the country. Many work in commerce, government and service industries, and manufacturing. In general, they are educated and family-oriented.

THE LOWER CLASS This class includes urban laborers, factory workers, domestics, small farmers, sharecroppers, and copper and coal miners, as well as the many unemployed living in the cities. Lower-class families are tight-knit and traditionally provide aid to members of the family in need of assistance. Often, households are made up of people from several generations, many of whom are forced to work to keep food on the table for the entire family.

People at the harbor front in Puerto Montt in the Lake District.

DRESS STYLES

Most Chileans dress like North Americans, though never as informally as the most casual Americans or as formally as the best-dressed Americans. Chileans generally do not wear shorts to do errands on weekends or gowns or tuxedos to weddings.

Chileans usually wear shorts at the beach and nice jeans when they go shopping. The men wear conservative suits for social or business occasions; the women wear suits and high heels for business and dresses for social occasions. On the most formal occasions, Chilean men wear dark suits and ties, and Chilean women wear cocktail dresses. Teenagers follow fashion trends in the United States.

Appropriately dressed for a folk festival, with clever use of strong colors.

The most traditional Chilean outfit is that worn by the *huaso* ("WAH-soh"), or horseman, during a festival or rodeo, Chile's national sport. The *huaso* wear a flat-brimmed, flat-topped hat that originated in the Andalusian region of southern Spain and a bolero jacket covered with a *manta* ("MAHN-tah"), or poncho. The *manta*, often multi-colored, is known for its intricate design and fine craftsmanship.

The *huaso* also often wear black pinstriped pants, leather leggings, and short, pointed high-heeled boots with spurs. In the 18th century, Chilean spurs were known for their size and decorative quality. They were about six inches (15 cm) across and had up to 24 points. Today, the typical spur is only three or four inches (8 or 10 cm) across.

TRADITIONAL COSTUMES OF CHILE

Chilean rodeo performer in traditional flat-brimmed hat of black or brown, and the *manta*, a short version of the poncho. It features an ivy leaf design.

Cowboy (*huaso*) in light brown woolen poncho and dark blue corduroy breeches. Leather boots, a belt, and a gray felt hat add the finishing touches.

Mapuche woman in red woolen top, handwoven dark blue woolen blanket skirt, and wooden clogs. The large silver pendant, silver earrings, and headpiece show the influence of Incan culture.

Chilean rancher in handwoven woolen poncho and a straw sombrero, leather boots, and decorative spurs. The spurs are not used to rake the horse's flesh but are pressed flat against the animal's sides. The saddle consists of several layers of felt.

Mapuche man on horseback. Beneath the woolen blanket poncho, he wears a shirt and trousers of llama wool simply wrapped around the legs and pulled up under the belt. A black felt hat protects his head. A superb horseman, he has no need for such extras as boots, stirrups, or spurs. A felt saddle and a simple loop for the big toe are sufficient.

LIFESTYLE

CHILEANS ARE GENEROUS, friendly, honest, outgoing, warm, and good-natured. They appreciate beauty, but scorn ostentatiousness. They are serious about education, the arts, and politics and are more accepting of new and progressive ideas than their Latin American neighbors. Chileans are highly tolerant of foreigners, yet they cherish their own culture. They are polite without being stiff, proud without acting superior, dignified but not at all snobbish.

Family is of utmost importance. Leisure activities and social occasions often center on the family, and the family home is thought of as a sacred place. Unlike many other Latin Americans, Chileans open up their homes to foreigners, and guests are made to feel like part of the family.

Like most Latin Americans, Chileans like to take their time about things. In Chile, one need never apologize for tardiness. It is customary to

arrive 15 minutes late for a small dinner party and 30 minutes late for a large party. However, it is not acceptable to be late for a business appointment. Businesspeople spend a good amount of time in casual conversation before the first meeting with a new client. Typical Chileans dislike forwardness and aggressiveness of any kind. They like to know someone fairly well before discussing personal or sensitive matters.

Opposite: **The Valdivia quayside shows a strong German influence.**

Above: **A middle-class Chilean family at Sunday lunch.**

LIFE IN SANTIAGO

Nearly 40 percent of all Chileans live in Santiago, the seventh largest city in Latin America. Santiago is the home of both the wealthiest and the poorest of Chilean society. Santiago is the cultural and intellectual hub of the country, the place where trends are set and where things happen. The city center is the location of government buildings, shops, hotels, offices, and movie theaters. During rush hour, traffic congestion is serious, and in the winter months, the smog is so bad that people wear surgical masks in the streets.

An affluent neighborhood in Santiago.

In the late 18th century, Santiago had a population of only about 30,000, nearly 90 percent of whom lived on farms in the countryside. By the early 19th century, the city had 100,000 inhabitants, good roads and railways had been built, and the colonial aristocracy had moved in.

Between 1865 and 1875, the population of the capital increased to 150,000 due to mass migration from the countryside. This trend continued well into the 20th century, because of people's inability to find employment in rural areas. The city did not always provide jobs either, although that fact did not deter many migrants.

Originally, migrants were forced to live in slums or tenements. Then they began to build makeshift homes on the unused land just outside the city. These came to be known as *poblaciones callampas* ("poh-blah-see-OH-ness kah-YAHM-pahs"), or mushroom villages. The dwellings were usually made from cardboard and tin. Few had running water, but many

A problem of the past. Chile's poor no longer have to live in shanty-towns. Just about all Chileans live in housing with water and electricity.

had electricity illegally drawn from power lines. Water came from a common faucet.

Beginning in the 1960s, the government made efforts to improve the living conditions in the *callampas* or to move the inhabitants to better housing. The Pinochet government initiated massive low-income housing programs, ranging from small apartments in four-story buildings to houses and plots of land with the most basic facilities. These housing projects were improved by the democratic governments that followed, but overcrowding, poor safety, and a lack of social facilities continue to plague the residents.

Santiago's upper class lives in large and luxurious apartments or homes in the *barrio alto* ("BAH-ree-oh AHL-toh"), the upper-class neighborhood. Some of these homes are modern, others are in the colonial style, complete with courtyard and tiled roof. Many have gardens and terraces that provide spectacular views of the city or the nearby Andean mountain range.

In the upper-middle-class home, the kitchen is the domain of the maid or maids who cook and clean for their employers. In many families, the mother rarely visits the kitchen; she plans the menu for the family and writes the shopping list, but she does not do the cooking.

A typical house in southern Chile.

RURAL HOUSING

A *ruca*, the traditional Mapuche house.

Although many Mapuche live in modern housing, some still live in traditional dwellings called *rucas* ("ROO-kahs"), found primarily in farmland near the city of Temuco. The low walls are wooden and the roof is thatched and comes to a peak. Inside, there is an earthen floor, often covered with a beautiful handmade rug; a fireplace that serves as both heat source and stove top; and sacks of potatoes and corn leaning against the walls.

The traditional Chilean rural house has long, dark corridors leading to large rooms with high ceilings; a large kitchen; and nearby stables. Some of the grander homes have their own orchards and even a small vineyard. Tenant farmers usually live in one-room adobe houses.

LIFE IN THE COUNTRY

The typical rural family in Chile probably lives and works on a farm, or *fundo*, in the country's fertile Central Valley. The average day on the *fundo* begins at dawn, when the family goes to the barn to milk the cows. At about 9 A.M., they sit down to a breakfast of rolls and coffee.

A house on stilts in Chiloé, southern Chile.

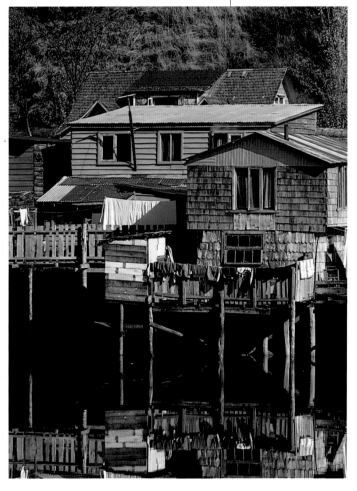

The day will be filled with the many demanding tasks related to cultivating crops and raising animals. Fresh meat and vegetables are normally purchased at a nearby outdoor market. In some cases, the farm may be near a major city, so the shopping can be done at a supermarket. Other farms may be very isolated, and trips to the local market are less frequent.

Children go to school at the same time as children in the cities, either in the morning or afternoon.

On Sundays, the family goes to Mass together. The meal following the Mass is the most elaborate of the week and is shared by cousins, aunts, uncles, and grandparents. After lunch, the children might go horseback-riding or spend time watching television or reading.

GENDER ROLES

Like most other Latin American countries, Chile is a male-dominated society. Men are expected to provide financial security for the family. Women have to take care of the home and raise the children, often while working outside the home as well.

Relationships in Chile are often very serious and casual dating is not the norm. Chileans tend to marry in their early 20s. When a man and woman marry, they start their family immediately. Middle-class families tend to be small, while wealthy and poor families are larger. Men are not likely to help out in domestic chores, even if they are unemployed. At meals, their wives serve them before the rest of the family.

Chilean children have a sense of duty toward their parents and often live at home until they marry. When they do leave home, they usually live in the same town or village, come home on Sundays and important holidays, and maintain a close relationship with their parents. Chilean parents tend to be very protective of their children. They tend to have a great deal of influence and are involved in their children's lives even when their children have families of their own.

Chileans are not as rigid in their interpretation of gender roles as other Latin Americans can be. Chilean women from all social classes are employed outside the home, either by necessity or by choice. They work in many sectors of the economy, as teachers, nurses, domestics, office workers, social workers, journalists, doctors, and lawyers.

Women in Chile were very active in political activities during the period of military rule. They marched in peace rallies carrying signs that said, "We want liberty—we don't want torture!" and braving tear gas and water cannons. They organized themselves into protest groups, campaigned for women's rights, established soup kitchens and schools in the shantytowns, and put pressure on the government to provide information on the whereabouts of their missing family members. For example, a group of women performed the national dance, the *cueca* ("KWAY-kah"), without the required male partner, as a way of bringing attention to their missing loved ones and the government that took them away.

An International Women's Day rally in Santiago. Women in Chile are politically active and do not hesitate to take on the government when they feel their rights have been abridged.

THE CHILEAN LIFE CYCLE

The important events in the life of a typical Chilean are performed in the Catholic or Evangelical Church.

WEDDINGS Chileans are not given to flashy displays of wealth; they tend to celebrate important occasions in a modest, dignified manner. Weddings, for instance, are rarely formal affairs. Chilean brides do not have bridesmaids or attendants to walk before them down the aisle. The bride is escorted only by her father, who hands her to the groom as they reach the altar. During the ceremony, which can be a brief 20-minute service or

Chilean weddings are usually not lavish, although much effort is put into making them enjoyable for all the guests.

a full hour-long Mass, the parents of the bride stand next to her and the parents of the groom next to him.

Wedding parties are usually held at home or in a small hall adjoining the church. Wine and champagne are served with the wedding dinner. This often consists of a very simple meal of meat, rice, salad, and cake. Usually there is dancing after dinner, with children and the elderly joining in. Afterward, the couple leaves for the honeymoon; popular locations are Viña del Mar, Rio de Janeiro, or Buenos Aires. Members of the upper class might go as far as Europe or the United States.

FUNERALS These are also simple events. The body of the deceased is sometimes kept at home for a couple of days before the religious ceremony. During this time, friends and relatives visit to provide comfort to the bereaved and to say prayers for the soul of the deceased. There is often just a brief memorial church service, followed by a short grave-side prayer. Few people wear black to funerals in Chile any more, although traditionally, a widow was expected to wear dark clothing for several months after the death of her husband.

CHILDHOOD

Chilean girls do not have fancy parties to celebrate their 15th birthday the way girls do in most other Latin American countries. In Chile, children's birthday parties are quite modest. Chilean children usually wear nice clothes to birthday parties, where they play and eat cake and ice cream. Parties at the homes of wealthier Chileans may have a hired clown or a puppet show for entertainment. Parties may also be held at fast-food restaurants such as McDonald's.

The most significant rites of passage are baptism, First Communion, marriage, and death. Even the Chilean who rarely attends Sunday Mass follows these traditions.

THE EDUCATIONAL SYSTEM

Chileans are very committed to education, and their educational system, based on French and German models, is highly regarded among Latin Americans. Getting a good education is a priority for the lower and middle classes as they seek to improve their living standards. Many Chilean social reformists are also passionate about providing a good education for all Chileans, regardless of their social class.

There are three types of schools in Chile: public, private (many of which are religious), and privately run but publicly funded (these do not charge their students tuition).

In 1880, urban children were given free, compulsory education; in 1920, the same was done for rural children. Now children are required to attend eight years of primary school and can go on to four years of

Free compulsory education gives Chile's poor the chance to improve their situation. Over 87 percent of all Chilean children are enrolled in primary school.

secondary or vocational school. After secondary school, those who qualify can go on to university for their degree courses.

The typical primary school curriculum consists of subjects such as mathematics, Spanish, English, art, science, and physical education. The optional secondary school course has two curricula: an arts and sciences program to prepare children going to college; and a vocational program to teach job skills.

Chile's universities are held in high regard throughout the region. The University of Chile, established in 1738, is the main university in the country. Its students are traditionally made up of members of the middle and lower classes. The private Catholic University in Santiago has been linked to the elite. There are universities in every major city. The University of Concepción and the University Austral of Valdivia are two well-known schools. There is also a growing number of smaller private universities.

RELIGION

RELIGION IS AN ELEMENT of Chilean culture that unites the people. Nearly 80 percent of Chileans are Roman Catholics. Just under 10 percent are Protestants, most belonging to fundamentalist churches. The Mapuche Indians have their own system of beliefs, and the rest of the population are Jewish, Muslim, Buddhist, or followers of the Baha'i faith.

Only about 25 percent of Chilean Catholics attend Mass regularly. Those between 11 and 20 years of age attend Mass still less frequently. Despite a lack of formal participation in church activities, however, Chileans consider themselves to be a Catholic people.

Young Chileans see going to Mass as both a religious and social event. About one-third of them attend Catholic schools, where they are immersed in the teachings of the Church. Many Chilean youths say prayers at night before they go to bed.

Chilean Catholics are generous in helping the less fortunate. Chile is probably the most dedicated Latin American country in implementing social reforms. The Chilean clergy has a history of social concern and progressive thought. Chile's most beloved priest, Father Alberto Hurtado (1902–1952), took in homeless children and started the country's most important charity, Hogar de Cristo. He has been beatified, and once canonized, he will become Chile's second saint, after Saint Teresa de los Andes, who was canonized in 1993. Many clergymen support family-planning programs and participate actively in programs to help the very poor.

Opposite: **A Chilean child taking part in Cuasimodo, a religious festival.**

Below: **Children in Chile are very involved in Catholic ceremonies.**

Worship at shrines is commonplace. Chileans may make a pilgrimage to one, as to the Virgin's shrine, or pray at roadside shrines.

RELIGION AND SOCIAL CLASS

Historically, the urban upper classes and wealthy landowners had a close relationship with the Church, so that the two influenced each other. On the other hand, the working class had neither the time nor the money to learn the teachings of Catholicism through formal education. They often became attached to one or more saints or believed in the magical powers of inanimate objects. Most lower-class Chileans, however, turn to the Church for the important rites of baptism, First Communion, marriage, and burial.

During the period of military rule, more Chileans drew closer to the Church. This happened because a part of the Church took a firm stand against the government, especially against its tendency toward violence and its harsh economic policies. The Catholic Church was responsible for

76

establishing and overseeing a broad range of social programs for the families of political prisoners and for the poor. These included school lunch programs for 30,000 children in Santiago, vocational training for adults, and assistance to small farmers and the unemployed.

Pinochet had some clergy members arrested and some exiled. The Church did not escape Pinochet's grip, but it did give the military government a force to reckon with.

Youth pray during the papal visit to Santiago in 1987.

CHURCH AND STATE

The 1925 constitution provided for freedom of religion and gave the Church independence from the State. The distance between them continued to widen during the military period.

In the mid-1970s, Cardinal Raúl Silva Henríquez established an organization called the Vicariate of Solidarity, a group of full-time lawyers and volunteers dedicated to defending victims of human rights abuses. The organization also provided counseling for victims and their families and set up workshops in which the wives and mothers of the tortured and the "disappeared" could make *arpilleras* ("are-pee-YEH-ras"), or embroidered tapestries depicting scenes from everyday life, to be sold to the public.

CATHOLIC BELIEFS AND TRADITIONS

Roman Catholics believe that the Pope is the leader of the Church and that his decisions are infallible. Also, Catholics receive a series of sacraments to nourish their spiritual life.

The first sacrament is baptism, when infants are cleansed of their "original sin." In Chile, children are baptized when they are about six months old. Parents invite family members to witness the ceremony and friends to celebrate with them at home after the ceremony. Godparents are appointed before the baptism; they promise to raise the child and oversee his or her religious education in the event of the parents' deaths.

The sacrament of First Communion is the child's introduction to receiving the body and blood of Christ in the form of bread and wine. Chilean children receive their First Communion in the eighth year, often on the Feast of the Immaculate Conception on December 8. They attend religious school to prepare for their First Communion, which is usually a group ceremony. Girls dress in white gowns like little brides, and boys wear suits. After the ceremony, the family gathers at home for a modest celebration. A second set of godparents is often chosen before the First Communion. Some parents allow their children to make the selection.

Marriage is also a sacrament. A church wedding is a sacred religious event. According to Catholic beliefs, marriage is a spiritual union that allows a couple to have children; it cannot be broken.

Another sacrament is the Anointing of the Sick. This is a rite of healing that can also be used as spiritual preparation for those who are dying. The priest puts olive oil—a symbol of light, strength, and life—on the forehead of the sick or dying person and asks for forgiveness of sins. The application of the holy oil serves two functions: it can help the sick person recover or, in terminal cases, prepare the soul for death.

A Catholic child's First Communion is a major milestone in her spiritual life.

First Communion is an important event, because it indicates that the child is now able to confess his or her sins and to receive the body and blood of Christ.

PROTESTANTS

About 10 percent of Chileans are Protestants. They may be Lutherans, mostly of German ancestry, Seventh Day Adventists, Baptists, or Methodists.

Pentecostalism, which is a form of Protestantism, is a growing movement in South America, especially in Brazil and Chile. Pentecostals believe in expressing themselves during the service, aloud or through body movements. Although they tend to be apolitical, they are committed to social reform. In 1986, for instance, they were involved in helping the Mapuche Indians retain their land.

The Pentecostal Methodist Church of Chile is one of the largest national Pentecostal churches in the world. It organizes a grand thanksgiving service every year in the Evangelical Cathedral of Santiago, which has a seating capacity of approximately 15,000 people. Evangelical pastors, leaders, and brothers gather to thank God for the country's independence and for the people's right to congregate in the denomination of their choice. Those in attendance also pray for the leaders and public servants of the country. In 1997, it was established that this annual thanksgiving service be one of the four official acts of the government to commemorate Chile's independence.

THE MAPUCHE TRADITION

The Mapuche have a very deep spirituality, based on the belief that there are positive and negative forces at work in everything. The east represents the positive forces, so all Mapuche homes face east. The Mapuche god is called Ngenechen, which means "master of the land." He is responsible for controlling nature, creating man and animals, and heading a pantheon of other gods who represent the sun, moon, stars, earth, sea, and thunder.

Opposite: **A Mapuche holy man near Temuco.**

To the Mapuche, the forces of evil, which bring floods, famine, and disease, are embodied in Wekufu, who fought unsuccessfully against Ngenechen to wipe out the ancestors of the Mapuche.

The Mapuche consult a medicine woman or *machi* ("MAH-chee") to cure sickness, to save a failing crop, or to receive a blessing. Only the *machi* can make contact with Ngenechen when she enters into a trance.

MYTHS OF CHILOÉ ISLAND

Chiloé Island, a community of fishermen, is steeped in folkloric tradition. Inhabitants of Chiloé believe in Pincoya, a creature that is half-human, half-fish. This protector of all seas is said to live in Lake Huelde on the island and to dance on the shore when the moon is full. If Pincoya dances facing the hills, the Chiloé fishermen's catch will be good.

The Chiloé Islanders also believe in a phantom ship, the Caleuche, that seduces sailors on board and then forces them to sail forever.

Chiloé Island is also known for its exquisite churches, some more than 200 years old.

A church on Chiloé Island.

MYTHICAL BELIEFS

The Mapuche, like many South American Indian peoples, believe in mythical animals that can perform extraordinary feats. A beast called a *cuero* ("koo-AY-roh") is a squid with many sets of eyes. It seizes swimmers, drags them under the surface, and eats them. The *camahueto* ("kah-mah-WAY-toh") is a huge seahorse that can destroy ships. Magicians ride on *camahuetos* when they travel. A fear of sorcerers, witches, and devils is common among the Mapuche. Diseases are said to be caused by evil spirits that possess the body or by enemies who cast spells.

LANGUAGE

SPANISH IS THE OFFICIAL LANGUAGE of Chile. Virtually everyone in the country speaks Spanish. Chile's rather isolated geography and its Spanish heritage have contributed to the creation of a homogeneous society with shared customs and values and a common language.

The Mapuche are the largest group of Chileans with a non-Spanish culture. They usually speak their own language, Mapudungun, though they also speak Spanish. The Aymara Indian language is spoken by a small group of people in the north. The inhabitants of Easter Island speak Rapa Nui, a Polynesian language, as well as Spanish. Some of the German, Italian, Palestinian, British, Croatian, and Korean immigrants speak their own languages at home and Spanish outside their homes.

Chileans who travel extensively, work in international firms, or whose jobs bring them in contact with tourists, speak English, but the vast majority of Chileans do not. Chileans appreciate foreigners who make an attempt to speak Spanish no matter how limited their knowledge of the language may be. Chileans generally love talking to foreigners and prefer poor communication to none at all.

Opposite: **A newspaper and magazine kiosk in Santiago sells mostly Spanish publications.**

Below: **This vendor in Valparaíso overcomes language barriers with graphics.**

CHILEAN SPANISH

The type of Spanish spoken in Chile differs from region to region and from social class to social class. As in most cultures, the educated upper social classes are likely to speak a more refined version of the language than the lower social classes.

Throughout Latin America, people who live at high altitudes tend to sound more clipped; they articulate their consonants but tend to drop their vowels. People who live in the lowlands often do just the opposite; they relax their consonants and retain their vowels. Hence, in Chile, the "s" at the end of a word is often dropped, or pronounced like an "h." *Las mamas* sounds like *la mamah*, and *los hombres* like *loh hombreh*. *Empanada* comes out as *empana'a*.

Whatever their geographic region or social level, Chileans are known for speaking extremely fast. This causes whole sounds or syllables to drop off completely: *hasta luego* ("so long") becomes *'stalugo*, and *dedo* ("finger") becomes *deo*. Non-Chileans who speak perfect *castellano*, the purist form of Spanish from Spain, may have difficulty following Chilean Spanish and vice versa.

A Chilean can pick out another Chilean in a crowd of Spanish-speaking people from different countries just by his or her pronunciation, use of slang, or speech patterns. Chileans tend to use the particle *re* ("reh") before certain words that they wish to emphasize. "Of course" might come out sounding like *"Rrrrr-claro!"* and "How pretty!" like *"Rrrrrreh lindo!"* In addition, Chileans love to end words with the suffix *-ito* or *-ita*, which means "little." This explains why a grown woman named Gloria might still be called Glorita by a good friend as a term of affection. Chileans often use the Italian word for goodbye, *ciao* ("CHOW"), instead of the Spanish *adiós* ("ah-dee-OHS").

BASIC CHILEAN PRONUNCIATION

SOUND/LETTER	PRONUNCIATION
f, k, l, m, p, t, y, ch	as in the English language
a	**a** as in "mark"
e	**a** as in "make" or **e** in "let"
i	**ee** as in "meet"
o	**o** as in "tot" or "lot"
u	**oo** as in "toot"
y	**ee** as in "meet"
b	resembles a **v** when placed between vowels
c	**s** as in "sink" when before **e** or **i**; or like **k** in "kite"
d	resembles **th** when at the end of a word
g	like **ch** in "loch" before **e** and **i**; or like **g** in "girl"
h	silent
j	**wh** as in "who"
ll	**y** as in "yes"
ñ	**ny** as in "canyon"
qu	**k** as in "kite"
r	rolled, especially at the beginning of a word
rr	strongly rolled
s	often dropped at the end of a word
v	**b** as in "bird"
x	**x** as in "taxi;" or **s** as in "sink" before a consonant
z	**s** as in "sink"

Chilean slang words and idioms distinguish them from other Latin Americans. For instance, they often use the phrase "al tiro" when they mean "immediately."

NONVERBAL COMMUNICATION

Chileans gesticulate when they speak, but not in an aggressive or confrontational manner. In 1985, when Chilean film director Miguel Littín entered Chile disguised as a Uruguayan businessman to make a movie about life under Pinochet, he had to consciously avoid making expressive hand gestures when speaking, or he would have given himself away.

As with many Latin Americans, Chileans touch one another in a dignified manner when greeting. Women friends follow the European custom of kissing each other on one cheek when they meet. Men friends shake hands; if they are good friends, they will also pat each other on the back. Men and women kiss once on the cheek at social events and shake hands in business situations. At small gatherings, it is polite to greet and say goodbye to every guest; a "hello" is acceptable at large parties.

Chileans generally do not stare at people when walking down the street or riding on the bus. They prefer not to make eye contact.

Right: **If a Chilean holds his hands up, palms outward and fingers apart, he means someone is stupid. Clenching the fist and raising it to eye level is a Communist sign, and standing with both arms raised is a sign of protest.**

Opposite: **If the hand is free, it is used to add emphasis to the words.**

SPANISH NAMES AND TITLES

Chileans follow the Spanish custom of using double surnames. A man named Carlos Rojas Pérez is addressed as Señor Rojas. Rojas is his father's surname, and Pérez is his mother's maiden name. If he marries a woman named Rosa Montalvo García, she does not change her name. Their children will take the first surnames of their father and mother. Thus they will have the surname Rojas Montalvo. Men and women are usually addressed as *Señor* or *Señora*. As a sign of respect, older people are called by their first name and an honorific, such as Don Carlos or Señora Rosa. In fact, if you meet the president, you could call him Don Ricardo.

Spanish culture and language, shared by the majority of Chileans, are preserved and strengthened by a wide range of publications in Spanish.

Easter Island is home to a Polynesian community that once had its own language and script.

THE RONGO-RONGO TABLETS

The ancient people of Easter Island, a small Polynesian territory that belongs to Chile, had their own language and a script that resembled Egyptian hieroglyphics. In 1864, a European missionary on the island noticed that many of the locals had wooden boards, called *rongo-rongo* tablets, on the walls of their homes. These were covered with small pictures of plants, animals, geometric shapes, and celestial beings that had been carved in rows using sharp stones. Even at that time, the islanders could not decipher the tablets.

According to legend, the ancient ruler of the Easter Islanders, Hotu Matua, brought the tablets to the island in A.D. 450. There were tablets for hymns, crimes, and historical events. Experts have had little luck deciphering the script on the few tablets that still exist on the island. Some believe that the characters do not represent an alphabet, because there are too many of them, but that they tell some sort of story. Others believe that the pictures are not a script at all, but serve as hints to help people remember important verses.

ARTS

CHILEANS ARE AN INTELLECTUAL PEOPLE who have great respect for education and the arts. Santiago, the capital, is the center of cultural expression in the country. It is home to the Museum of Pre-Columbian Art, which contains ancient Latin American artifacts; the Fine Arts Museum, with its excellent collection of Chilean paintings; and the Municipal Theater, where Chileans go to see the Ballet de Santiago, the Philharmonic Orchestra, and the opera. There is also the San Francisco Church and Museum, which contains an impressive collection of religious art and antiques. The city home of Nobel prize-winning Chilean poet Pablo Neruda is also in Santiago and is open to the public, as is the Cousino Palace, an 1871 mansion filled with European antiques and decorations.

Opposite: **Statue in front of the Fine Arts Museum in Santiago.**

Above: **German costume, dance, and music are the tradition in Valdivia.**

Chilean artists such as surrealist painter Roberto Matta and sculptor Marta Colvin are internationally recognized. An important Chilean classical musician is pianist Claudio Arrau, who was one of the finest interpreters of the works of Beethoven. Chilean composers Enrique Soro and Juan Orrego are well known among Latin Americans. The *Nueva Canción*, or New Song, movement began in Chile in the 1960s and spread to all of Latin America. Led by musician and poet Violeta Parra, the movement concerned itself with social protest and labor reform. It was filled with the revolutionary spirit of the time.

Youths paint a mural of Allende.

POLITICS AS INSPIRATION

During Pinochet's rule, many of Chile's finest artists—filmmakers, poets, novelists, theater directors, fabric artists, musicians, and songwriters—expressed their disapproval of the political situation through their art. Artistic and intellectual life was severely repressed. Many artists chose to leave Chile; others were exiled.

The art created by Chileans abroad during this period is often concerned with the loss of homeland and the tragedy of a people stifled by a repressive government. Those who remained in Chile also expressed their dissatisfaction with the regime by creating "protest art."

MIGUEL LITTÍN: CLANDESTINE IN CHILE

Chile's leading film director and Academy Award nominee, Miguel Littín, was permanently exiled from his homeland by General Pinochet in 1973. After living in Mexico and Spain for more than 10 years, he returned to Chile in 1985, disguised as a Uruguayan businessman, to shoot an undercover film about life under Pinochet. Nobel prize-winning novelist Gabriel García Márquez told Littín's story in a fascinating, suspense-filled book entitled *Clandestine in Chile: The Adventures of Miguel Littín.*

In his book *Clandestine in Chile*, Colombian-born writer Gabriel García Márquez wrote a fascinating account of Littín's experiences during the making of a film in Chile .

To enter Chile undetected, Littín had to adopt a whole new persona. He learned to speak with a Uruguayan accent and to change his characteristic laugh and walk. He lost weight, shaved off his beard, colored his hair, and gave up his jeans for a stiff business suit. He was so convincing that his own mother did not recognize him when he returned home to his village!

While in Chile, Littín and his underground allies directed more than five different film crews working simultaneously at different locations. The result was some 100,000 feet (30,480 m) of film—some shot right in the office of General Pinochet—that was ultimately edited into a two-hour feature film. When García Márquez's book was published in Spanish, Pinochet impounded and burned 15,000 copies in Valparaíso.

A mural in Santiago dedicated to Nobel prize-winning poet Gabriela Mistral.

POETRY

Poetry is a dominant art form in Chile. In the 16th century, Spanish poet Alonso de Ercilla y Zúñiga published an epic poem called *La Araucana* about the battles between the Spanish and the Mapuche. The poem is considered Chile's first major literary work and is widely read and memorized by schoolchildren.

Gabriela Mistral, or *la divina* ("the divine") Gabriela, as she is called by Chileans, was born Lucila Godoy Alcayaga in Vicuña in 1889. She was a poor but educated rural schoolteacher. She wrote honest, passionate poetry about her village, children, and the loss of love (her lover killed himself when she was 20). Her first volume of poems was published in 1922. Called *Desolación* (Desolation), it was about pain and death. *Ternura* (Tenderness), published in 1925, celebrated birth and motherhood.

Mistral also wrote about love, religion, nature, and justice.

Mistral's poetry is beautiful, compassionate, and shows a special love for the common country people. As a result, people of all classes adored her. In 1945, she became the first Latin American to receive a Nobel prize in literature. The judges honored her "for her lyric poetry, which is inspired by powerful emotions and which has made her name a symbol of the idealistic aspirations of the entire Latin American world." When she died in 1957, the Chilean government declared three days of official mourning. Her poems have been translated into English, French, German, and other languages.

Poet Pablo Neruda, whose real name was Neftalí Reyes Basoalto, received a Nobel prize in literature in 1971. Neruda's early poems dealt with love and nature. His most famous work is *Twenty Love Poems and a Song of Despair*. He was an advocate of the poor, and his later work was highly political.

A confirmed communist, Neruda was a friend and ally of Marxist President Salvador Allende. He composed verse about poverty, hunger, and the plight of the factory worker. Neruda died just weeks after Pinochet came to power and later became a symbol of the artistic freedoms that were lost under the new regime. Chileans have flocked to the village of Isla Negra, where he lived, to scratch messages of hope into the fence surrounding his cliff-top home. "Always you are present and in the thoughts of the people," says one. Since Neruda's house was opened to the public, a month after the democratic government took power, many exiled poets and intellectuals have visited to pay their respects.

Much of the poetry written in Chile after Neruda's death revolved around the political situation at the time. Since many published literary works were censored, a great deal of the poetry written in the 1970s and

"Little children's feet, blue from the cold, how can they see you and not cover you, dear God!"

—*Gabriela Mistral*

"This night is the same night; it whitens the same trees; casts similar shadows; it is as dark, as long, as deep, and as endurable. As any other night. It is true: I do not want her."

—*Pablo Neruda*

1980s was read aloud in cafés or at the meetings of literary groups, or published in makeshift magazines. Leading poets from this period and from the present include Diego Maqueira and Raúl Zurita.

NOVELS

While Chilean poets are known for their extraordinary talent, most Chilean novelists have neither received as much international recognition nor developed as distinct a literary voice to separate them from other Latin American writers. Isabel Allende and José Donoso are two exceptions.

Isabel Allende, Salvador Allende's niece, left Chile to live in Venezuela after Pinochet's takeover. There, she wrote her first novel, *La casa de los espíritus* (House of the Spirits), which tells the story of an aristocratic Chilean family ruled by a violent, autocratic, and passionate patriarch, Estéban, and his tender, clairvoyant wife, Clara. Based loosely on Allende's own childhood experiences, the novel is characteristic of the 20th-century Latin American novel, full of vivid, fantastical stories that place magical characters against a backdrop of a politically volatile and violent society. Translated into English, *La casa de los espíritus* became a bestseller in Europe and the United States. It was also made into a film.

Isabel Allende's subsequent novels, *De amor y de sombra* (Of Love and Shadow) in 1984 and *Eva Luna* in 1987, both met with critical acclaim worldwide. A collection of short stories, *Cuentos de Eva Luna* (Stories of Eva Luna), followed in 1990, and *El plan infinitivo* (The Infinite Plan) in 1991. In 1995, Isabel Allende wrote *Paula*, a story about the death of her daughter. In 1999, she published *Daughter of Fortune*.

Literary critics in Europe and throughout Latin America consider novelist José Donoso one of Chile's finest authors. Translated into many languages, Donoso's books are about such subjects as the decadence of

**Isabel Allende, author of
the bestselling novel
House of the Spirits.**

the elite, aging, sickness, and childhood demons. His novels are strikingly real and yet magical; *Desesperanza* (Curfew) and *El jardín de al lado* (Garden Next Door) deal with politically charged topics such as exile. Donoso died in 1996 in Santiago at the age of 71.

WRITERS IN EXILE

Donoso believed that many of the more recent Latin American novels resembled one another because their authors were living in exile when they wrote their novels. Isabel Allende was in Venezuela writing about Chile; Gabriel García Márquez was in Mexico writing about Colombia; Mario Vargas Llosa was in Paris writing about Peru; and José Donoso, himself, was either in Europe or in the United States writing about Chile.

TODA PERSONA ACUSADA DE DELITO
TIENE DERECHO A QUE SE PRESUMA
SU INOCENCIA

"Any person accused of a crime has the right to be presumed innocent," reads this *arpillera*.

These novelists painted the Latin American political and social landscape, as they saw it, in their stories. The price they had to pay to do this was exile. Even in colonial times, Brazilian poets were banished to Angola. Today, many younger Latin American writers live far from their homeland, but continue to write about the concerns of their home countries.

FOLK ART

ARPILLERAS One of the finest expressions of Chilean folk art is the *arpillera* ("are-pee-YEH-rah"), a wall hanging done on burlap or sackcloth that depicts scenes from everyday life. The pictures are made using bright-colored embroidery thread and scraps of old material.

Arpilleras are also made in other South American countries, but in Chile they had special political significance. Many Chilean *arpilleras* were created by a group of 600 women whose husbands were killed or imprisoned during the military regime. The women sewed to feed their families and to voice their protest. Some *arpilleras* depict protest marches, candlelight vigils for political prisoners, or people voting to put General Pinochet out of office. Several books have been written about Chile's accomplished *arpilleristas*, as *arpillera* artists are called, and their craft is attracting international recognition.

Other Chilean *arpillera* masterpieces are made in Isla Negra, a small coastal village that was home to poet Pablo Neruda. A group of about 50 women—wives of farmers and fishermen—create apolitical *arpilleras* that depict charming scenes of the countryside and coastline, wheat-threshing celebrations, or fruit stands. The embroidered picture covers the entire cloth and can take up to a year to create. The tapestry makers in Isla Negra belong to a cooperative that furnishes some 900 different colors of yarn and oversees the quality of each *arpillera*.

Mapuche women have found a commercial outlet for their beautiful folk art.

CRAFTS The Mapuche of Chile make beautiful handwoven ponchos, blankets, and sweaters, which they sell in Temuco. The Mapuche are also known for their silver jewelry, pottery, and musical instruments like panpipes and drums.

Replicas of Diaguita pottery are sold in handicraft stores in Chile. Decorated with heads of llamas, birds, or black-and-white geometric designs over terracotta, Diaguita dishes and jugs display an elegant simplicity.

Pomaire, a town about 35 miles (56 km) southwest of Santiago, is known for its hand-molded pottery made from a dark clay scraped from the nearby mountains. The pieces of pottery are fired in large, old-fashioned kilns and then sold from the traditional adobe houses.

CUECA Most festivals and celebrations in Chile include the national folk dance, *cueca,* of which there are different regional styles. Inspired by the ritual of a rooster stalking a hen, it is the dance of courtship. A man dressed as a *huaso* and a woman in a full skirt, each holding a handkerchief, dance subtly and expressively around each other as musicians play the guitar, tambourine, harp, and accordion and the audience claps, shouts, and stamps their feet.

LEISURE

CHILEANS SPEND A LOT OF TIME with their families. On Sundays, many families gather to cook and share a large meal together after Mass. Then, they may play a game of cards or dominoes.

In wealthy urban families, weekends may be spent horseback riding, swimming, or playing golf or tennis. In the winter, wealthy Chileans may take ski vacations at prime resorts just an hour or two from Santiago. In the summer, they probably vacation at sea resorts along Chile's coast. Middle-class families also take beach vacations, and they enjoy camping in the parks and campgrounds of the Andes and the Lake District.

The middle-class *santiaguino* ("sahn-tee-ah-GEE-noh"), or resident of Santiago, may spend an evening out at one of the city's many restaurants and then go to a movie. The upper-class Chilean would host an elegant dinner party or go to the opera, the theater, or the ballet.

On weekends, teenagers from all classes congregate at the shopping mall, just as teenagers do in the United States. In Santiago, there are many multi-level shopping centers filled with shops that sell everything from French perfume to Japanese computer games. The city's teenagers go there to hang out in groups.

On Sundays, it is not unusual to see young couples walking hand-in-hand through Santiago's public parks. In spring, Chileans of all ages and social classes enjoy their national hobby—flying kites in Santiago's parks and fields.

Opposite: **An enlarged chess set provides mental—and physical—exercise for Chileans in Frutillar.**

Below: **Musicians entertain shoppers.**

105

SPORTS

Chileans are active participants in the same amateur sports that interest North Americans and Europeans. Chileans play tennis, golf, volleyball, basketball, polo, and rugby and enjoy bowling, horseback riding, jogging, snow skiing, fishing, scuba diving, and water skiing.

SOCCER As in the rest of Latin America, the favorite spectator sport in Chile is soccer, or *fútbol* ("FOOT-ball"). Chile hosts major international matches that attract some 80,000 people to Santiago's national stadium. Chile's finest professional soccer players are likened to national heroes and are instantly recognizable to nearly every Chilean.

Soccer is popular even as far out as the Juan Fernández Islands.

In the 1989 election that voted Pinochet out of office, soccer star Carlos Caszely appeared on television commercials with his mother, who had been unlawfully arrested during the Pinochet regime, and encouraged people to vote against the continuation of the military government. His appearance, according to many Chileans, was instrumental in swaying the vote against Pinochet.

In the country and the city, boys play soccer wherever they can: in the schoolyard, on the streets, in parks, and even at home.

Matches between schools or soccer clubs are very competitive. The fiercest rivalry is between the country's two best teams, the University of Chile team and the Colo-Colo team, named after a Mapuche chief.

SNOW SKIING The Andean mountain range close to Santiago and in the far southern provinces provides Chileans with ideal skiing country. The ski season (June to September or October) attracts thousands of South Americans to Chile's 14 ski centers.

Portillo is a world-famous ski resort about 100 miles (161 km) north of Santiago. The site of the 1966 World Championships, Portillo is said to have the finest competitive runs. Farellones, 30 miles (48 km) from Santiago, is another popular resort; some upper-class *santiaguinos* have weekend apartments up at Farellones. Resorts farther south, near Punta Arenas, are the only places in all of South America where skiers can see the ocean as they descend the slopes. Another ski center, Termas de Chillán, has the longest chairlift in South America, some of the best open-slope skiing in the Andes, and natural hot springs for after-ski bathing.

Valle Nevado, the newest and most lavish ski resort in Chile, is about 40 miles (64 km) northeast of Santiago. It even has facilities for heli-skiing, a combination of skiing and hang-gliding.

These hikers are dangerously close to a crevasse in the ice cap near the summit of Volcán Villarrica, an active volcano in the Lake District.

WATER SPORTS Chileans love the beach, and many make a pilgrimage to Viña del Mar each year to swim, tan, gamble at the casinos, walk in the famous gardens, or eat fresh seafood in one of the restaurants that overlook the ocean. During the peak of the summer season, the streets are filled with people shopping, searching out cafés, and riding in horse-drawn carriages called *victorias* ("veek-TOH-ree-ahs").

Deep-sea and lake fishing are also popular sports in Chile. In the north, people fish for tuna, bonito, swordfish, shark, and marlin; in the south, fishing for trout is quite common. Some of the best fishing in South America is done in the Lake District, about 320 miles (515 km) south of Santiago. Scuba diving, boating, and water-skiing are popular in many areas off the coast.

Jet skis on Lake Villarica in Pucon.

KITE FLYING In the 18th century, Catholic monks brought the first kites to Chile, and kite flying became an amusement for the upper classes. Today, *santiaguinos* from all walks of life fly kites for fun and for sport from September, the beginning of spring, until the weather turns cold again. Kites are sold for about a dollar at small stalls set up on Santiago's street corners.

Thousands of *santiaguinos* turn out each weekend to fly their kites in public parks, and the sky gets so dense with kites that it is difficult to tell one's kite from another. Many strings become intertwined, crossing and cutting one another, and a few kites may crash into trees and power lines.

Serious kite fliers belong to clubs like the Chilean Kite Fliers Association, which is divided into teams. In one type of competition, two five-member teams battle to snap the strings of all the opponents' kites. Kites dart across the sky, twirling, jumping, and diving to avoid their rivals. The string must be of white cotton and is sharpened with glass powder. Kite fliers often tape their fingers to avoid getting cut by the glass powder. Sometimes, two men handle one kite: one controls movement; the other releases string from the 1,000-yard (914-m) spool.

Kites have been honored in Chilean literature as a national treasure, and to some, they are as much a part of the country's folklore as are the rodeo, *cueca,* and *empanada* ("ehm-pah-NAH-dah"), a Chilean snack.

FLYING HIGH

On October 28, 1993, 9-year-old Augustín Ortíz piloted his family's single-engine plane all by himself. In doing so, he broke the Guinness world record for being the youngest pilot to fly solo. The previous record was held by an 11-year-old North American boy.

Chilean rodeo is a popular spectator sport because of its colorful costumes and fine horsemanship.

THE RODEO

Chilean rodeo, which has little in common with North American rodeo, has its roots in 16th-century colonial society and is still a much-loved leisure activity. The rodeo began when Spanish ranchers hosted annual cattle roundups in Santiago to show off their cattle-leading skills. Over time, the sport developed into a contest of skill and horsemanship with very specific rules. Today, the rodeo is the most popular sport after soccer.

Originally, teams of riders that competed in the rodeo were made up of landowners and their employees. Now the competing teams are made up of partners or friends, usually members of the upper and middle classes, who own farms and horses. Rodeo teams often travel from village to village with their families and stay in one another's homes. The teams are called *colleras* ("koh-YEH-ras"), and the horses receive as much recognition as the riders.

The rodeo

Also known as *la fiesta huasa* ("lah fee-ESS-tah WAH-sah"), the rodeo takes place in many towns throughout central and southern Chile in arenas called *media lunas* ("MEH-dee-ah LOO-nahs"), or half moons.

The competition begins when pairs of *huasos* enter the ring in pursuit of a young bull. The riders wear traditional *huaso* gear—flat-topped hats, colorful short-cropped ponchos, fringed leggings, and pointed boots with spurs—and equip their horses with festive saddles.

In the rodeo ring, the riders take up positions at the flank and rear of the bull. Their aim is to force the bull to stop, without using a lasso, at a certain place in the fence. Judges award points according to where the horse touches the bull: no points are given for a block on the neck, but two are given for the shoulder blade, three for behind the shoulder blade, and four for the back legs, the most difficult part for the horse to make a block on. The riders try three times on each of three bulls, changing their positions each time.

Although Chilean rodeo might sound a bit tame to fans of North American bronco-busting, it is quite entertaining to Chileans, who appreciate fine horsemanship. Riders occasionally do have a brush with danger, such as when they run into a frightened 800-pound (363-kg) bull.

Before the rodeo, it is customary to gather in a large shed outside the *media luna* to eat *empanadas* and drink good Chilean wine. After the event, the crowd cheers the winning riders, who receive trophies or certificates—no money—as prizes. After giving away the prizes, the crowd will gather round as the *huaso* dances the *cueca* with the rodeo queen and sings a *tonada* ("toh-NAH-dah")—a touching, sentimental song, that is the equivalent of a North American country ballad—about a lost love, sadness, or an emotional event.

Chileans come to the rodeo to watch a dignified sport that has contributeed significantly to their history and culture.

FESTIVALS

THE MOST COLORFUL FESTIVALS in Chile are religious in nature. They consist of a procession, a special Mass, and often a market for local crafts and produce. Folk dances are an important part of the festivities. These dances often display a combination of Spanish and Indian elements.

Patron saints' days are celebrated with small processions in which villagers carry images of the particular saint through the streets. In Antofagasta, the image of the patron saint of fishermen, San Pedro, is taken out in a boat to the breakwater to bless the first catch of the day. On the Feast of the Lady of Mount Carmel, schoolchildren, government officials, members of sports clubs, and other devotees pay homage to the patron lady of Chile.

Religious celebrations and processions can attract thousands of people not only to worship, but also to take part in the festivities.

Celebrations honoring Saint Isidore (patron saint of peasants in northern Chile), the Lady of Lo Vazquez, and Saint Sebastian are especially popular. Beside providing community solidarity, holidays and festivals in Chile are important family occasions.

Opposite: **Chileans celebrate Cuasimodo, a traditional festival held a week after Easter.**

OFFICIAL HOLIDAYS IN CHILE

Jan 1	New Year's Day	Sep 18	Independence Day
Apr	Holy (Easter) Week	Sep 19	Armed Forces Day
May 1	Labor Day	Sep	National Unity Day
May 21	Navy Day		(holiday on first Mon.)
Jun	Corpus Christi	Oct 12	Columbus Day
Jun 29	Feast of Saints Peter and Paul		(holiday on nearest Mon.)
	(holiday on nearest Mon.)	Nov 1	All Saints' Day
Aug 15	Assumption of	Dec 8	Immaculate Conception
	the Virgin Mary	Dec 25	Christmas Day

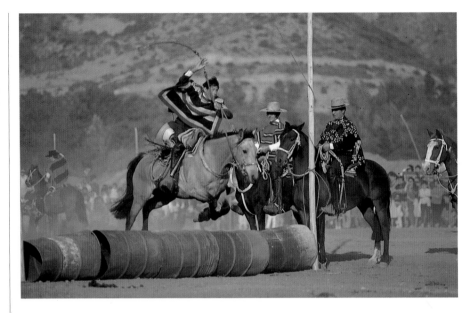

EASTER IN THE COUNTRYSIDE

A religious tradition unique to Chile is held in villages throughout central Chile on the Sunday after Easter. Called Domingo de Cuasimodo (taken from a Latin phrase used during the Easter service that refers to Christ's resurrection), the festival is celebrated with great fanfare. Houses are decorated, and members of the procession wear costumes and parade through the village on horseback, holding pennants and images of Christ. Families save for a year to decorate the carriages and floats they ride in during the procession. Horsemen don their finest *huaso* attire and drape their mounts in beautiful capes that resemble those worn by the horses of knights in the Middle Ages.

The festival has a fascinating history. In the 19th century, after Independence, groups of bandits terrorized rural communities outside Chile's larger cities. Outlaws like the Pincheira brothers, who ruled over territory south of Santiago, scared away even government troops. They stole valuables from farmers and sacred objects

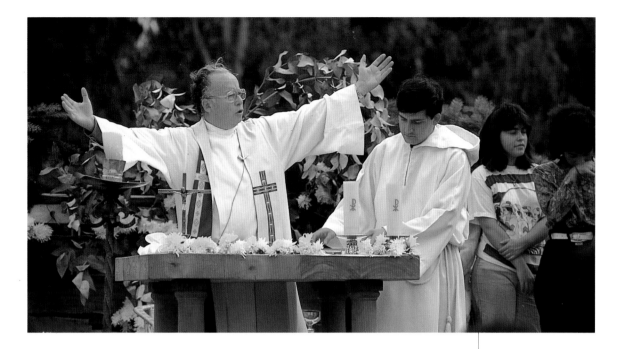

like gold cups and costly vestments from priests traveling to their parishes.

To protect the priests, armed *huasos* began to escort them on their travels. Dressed in bright-colored riding outfits, the *huasos* would storm through the countryside ahead of the procession, holding an image of Christ and daring the thieves to challenge them.

After the bandits were stopped, the festivity became a religious tradition as well as a chance to show off one's finest *huaso* garb. Today, ranchers and farmers "run the Cuasimodo" dressed in colorful cloaks and black trousers. Instead of wearing the traditional flat hat, they tie white handkerchiefs around their heads as a sign of respect. Their dress is Spanish in origin, but their reckless riding style is reminiscent of the Mapuche, who became expert horsemen in their battles against the Spaniards.

Riders escort priests who ride in decorated coaches. As they parade through the villages, the elderly and sick come to the doors and windows of their houses to receive Holy Communion. Men, women, and children follow the lead coach in horse-drawn coaches, floats, or—in towns where horses are not as readily available—on bicycles or motorcycles.

CHILEAN INDEPENDENCE DAY

Independence Day is a grand affair in Chile. This day provides Chileans the opportunity to demonstrate their fierce patriotism. All throughout the month of September, Chilean flags are flown in front of houses and mounted on cars.

On September 18, Chileans spend the day eating *empanadas* and drinking red wine and *chicha* ("CHEE-chah"), a fermented grape drink.

The next day, the 19th, the armed forces stage a large parade in Santiago, attended by the president and other government officials. Smaller parades are held in cities and villages throughout the country.

After the parades, people gather to dance the *cueca*. There are two types of outfits worn. In the simple version, men dress as *huasos* and women wear full calico skirts. In the more elegant version, men don a more refined *huaso* costume and women wear white ruffled blouses under cropped black jackets with a long narrow black skirt. The *cueca* symbolizes the ritual of courtship. Lively crowds clap and cheer the dancers on.

Independence Day celebrations are sometimes followed by a traditional Chilean rodeo event.

Log-splitting contests are part of a Chiloé Island festival.

116

Easter Islanders during the festival of Corpus Christi.

THE FESTIVAL OF LA TIRANA

Some 150,000 people gather in the village of La Tirana near the Atacama Desert to show devotion to the Virgin Mary each July. Many are members of dance and music clubs that come to honor the Virgin or to give their thanks for favors she has granted during the year.

The musicians play trumpets, trombones, cymbals, and drums in the middle of a group of dancers, who dance for three days straight, pausing only to eat and change their costumes. The dancers say that they need neither stimulants nor alcohol to keep going, because their faith spurs them on. After the dances, the performers make a pilgrimage to the church of the Virgen del Carmen.

The village of La Tirana, which means "The Tyrant," got its name from an Indian princess who, after being converted to Catholicism, became a tyrant in her efforts to convert the rest of her people. Her people murdered her for her disloyalty, but a priest later succeeded in converting them all. A sanctuary was built to honor the princess and the Virgin Mary. People have come to pray here ever since.

The "old man of Christmas" comes to the Plaza de Armas in Santiago with reindeer, sleigh, red robe, and a beach umbrella to protect him from Chile's summer sun.

CHRISTMAS IN CHILE

There are two major differences between Christmas in Chile and Christmas in North America. In Chile, Christmas arrives in the middle of summer and is, therefore, not associated with snowflakes, snowmen, and snow-covered trees. In addition, Christmas in Chile—and in much of Latin America—is more a religious celebration than a commercial holiday. Although large department stores decorate their windows, and Christmas trees, presents, and Santa Claus (called *Viejo Pascuero*, or "old man of Christmas") are common, the emphasis is still on the birth of Christ.

Christmas in Chile

In mid-December, many Catholic families set up nativity scenes at home. Some are very simple, with only small images of Joseph, Mary, the Christ child, and a cow; others are elaborate, featuring the countryside, the Three Wise Men, the angels, the shepherds, and many animals. In upper-class families, the nativity figures may be made of the finest materials and are passed down through generations. In poorer families, whose nativity figures may be made from clay or cardboard, the figure of Christ is often cast in porcelain. There are even nativity scenes that occupy whole rooms and include such props as grass, roads, hills, and tiny villagers. In Viña del Mar, famous full-scale nativity scenes are often set up in public places.

On Christmas Eve, Chileans attend a midnight Mass called *misa de gallo* ("MEE-sah deh GAH-yoh"), or Rooster's Mass, and have a sumptuous holiday supper afterward. Instead of turkey and stuffing, they eat lobsters. Some Chilean families go to restaurants to indulge in an unusual Mapuche specialty called *curanto* ("koo-RAHN-toh"). Chileans make this dish by digging a deep pit in the sand, lining it with herbs, leaves, and hot stones, and then filling it with layers of eggs, vegetables, seafood, poultry, and pork. More hot stones are placed on top, and the pit is covered tightly. Entire wheelbarrows of the dish are served to people seated outdoors.

An alcoholic drink called *cola de mono* ("KOH-lah day MOH-noh"), or "monkey's tail," is traditionally made during the Christmas season. It contains a powerful alcohol called *aguardiente* ("ah-gwahr-dee-EHN-teh"), coffee, milk, sugar, cinnamon, and egg yolk. A dry cake or bread full of candied fruits, called *pan de pascua* ("pahn day PAHS-kwah"), or "Christmas bread," is also a Chilean Christmas treat.

Chileans open their gifts when they return home from midnight Mass. Christmas Day is often a quiet family day, when relatives visit and exchange presents.

Unlike Christmas in North America, Christmas in Chile comes in summer, and Chileans eat lobster and drink coffee-flavored eggnog.

119

FOOD

A PROFUSION OF DELICIOUS FOODS can be found in Chilean markets. Fresh fruit like strawberries, raspberries, grapes, melons, bananas, figs, pears, apricots, and peaches abound. Fresh vegetables like corn, avocado, squash, potatoes, eggplant, garlic, carrots, peppers, and beans are plentiful. But most impressive are the seafood stalls, which overflow with a variety of fish and shellfish straight from local waters.

Chileans are a seafood-eating people. This is due to the lack of land for cattle-grazing and the fact that no city in Chile is far from the sea. Fresh fish is inexpensive, and all Chileans eat fish regularly. The icy cold Humboldt Current that flows north from Antarctica into the Pacific waters off Chile provides the country with some of the world's finest and most unusual fish. *Locos* ("LOH-kohs"), which are similar to abalone, *machas* ("MAH-chahs"), or razor clams, *erizos* ("eh-REE-sos"), which are sea urchins the size of tennis balls, *camarones* ("kah-mah-ROH-nehs"), or shrimp, *langostinos* ("lahng-gohs-TEE-nohs"), which are tiny rock lobsters, and *congrio* ("KON-gree-oh"), or conger eel, are Chilean favorites.

Opposite: **A comfortable seat at the central fruit market in Santiago.**

Below: **A riverside fish market in Valdivia.**

Chilean cuisine has both indigenous and European influences. For example, *porotos granados* ("poh-ROH-tols grah-NAH-dos"), a bean stew, combines indigenous ingredients such as corn, squash, and beans and distinctly Spanish ingredients such as onions and garlic. Another popular dish with indigenous influences is *humitas* ("ooh-MEE-tahs"). This is ground corn mixed with milk, basil, and onions. They are wrapped in corn husks and boiled. Meals are usually accompanied by Chilean wine.

CHILEAN SPECIALTIES

POROTOS GRANADOS Loved by all Chileans, this vegetarian stew is made of corn, beans, squash, onions, and garlic. The main ingredient, cranberry beans, is grown almost year-round in the central region, which has a mild, stable climate. If fresh cranberry beans are not available, dried cranberry or navy beans are a good substitute. Some Chileans eat the stew topped with a spoonful of *pebre* ("PEH-breh"), a hot sauce of onions, vinegar, olive oil, garlic, chili, and coriander.

EMPANADAS These pastries are stuffed with meat, cheese, or seafood. *Empanadas de pino* are filled with meat, onions, raisins, a black olive, and a hard-boiled egg. The turnovers are baked until the crust is lightly browned. Chileans eat *empanadas* as a snack or as the first course of the main meal, often with red wine. Heaps of *empanadas* are served at festivals and celebrations or at rodeos.

*Opposite: **Curanto**, a rich southern dish traditionally cooked in a pit dug into the ground and covered with hot rocks. Ingredients include beef, pork, chicken, lamb, potatoes, peas, beans, lobsters, mussels, oysters, and clams.*

Below: Raw seafood is a delicacy. Here, clams are relished with a squeeze of lemon juice and a buttered roll. Huge sea urchins are another delicacy, served raw with chopped herbs. The flesh is a shocking yellow-orange, and tiny crabs attached are eaten live.

CONGRIO Conger eel is a gourmet treat in Chile. It is not an eel, but a long, nearly boneless, firm-fleshed fish with a small tail. It can be baked, grilled, fried, or stewed. The fish comes in three varieties: black, gold, and red (the rarest and tastiest). *Caldillo de congrio* ("kahl-DEE-yoh deh KON-gree-oh"), a soup of conger eel, tomatoes, potatoes, onions, herbs, and spices, is a national dish. It is traditionally stewed in an earthen pot to seal in the seasoning and give it a hearty flavor.

ALCOHOLIC BEVERAGES

Chileans, like the French, are great wine drinkers. Chileans have wine at lunch and dinner, wine at the cocktail hour, and wine at home and in restaurants. Unlike other Latin Americans, Chileans do not add water to their wine.

Chilean wines are of high quality and are reasonably priced; they are a source of national pride. Some of the finest varieties sell for less than $2 a bottle in Chile and only about $5 in the United States. Wine critics liken Chilean wines to French rather than Californian wines in flavor. The best vineyards are found in the Central Valley, which has what is known as a Mediterranean climate—warm summer, dry autumn, and mild spring.

Harvesting grapes at a vineyard near Santiago, in the Central Valley.

Bottled wines in Chile are graded according to quality: *gran vino* ("gran VEE-noh") is good wine, *vino especial* ("ehs-peh-see-AHL") is better, and *vino reservado* ("reh-serh-VAH-doh") is the best. Red wine is called *vino tinto* ("TEEN-toh"); white wine is *vino blanco* ("BLAHN-koh"); dry is *seco* ("SEH-koh"); and sweet is *dulce* ("DOOL-say").

An extremely popular alcoholic drink in Chile, *pisco* ("PEES-koh"), is also made from grapes. Almost colorless, with a light fragrance, *pisco* does not appear strong, but it is. It can be served by itself, mixed with ginger ale, cola, or vermouth, or in its most loved form, as *pisco sour*—a frothy cocktail made with *pisco*, lemon juice, sugar, ice, and beaten egg white.

Chicha, a fermented grape-juice drink that tastes like apple cider, and *aguardiente*, or "fire water", a potent beverage distilled from grapes, are often served at holidays. *Chicha* is drunk at Independence Day celebrations.

OTHER BEVERAGES

Chile is not a coffee-drinking nation. A diner who orders *café* will get a cup of hot water and a small jar of instant coffee; coffee made from freshly ground beans is costly. Chileans order *café café* to get good, brewed coffee or *espresso*. A *café con leche* ("kah-FAY kon LEH-chay"), coffee with milk, is one spoonful of coffee in a cup of hot milk. In many European and South American countries, the mixture is half milk, half coffee.

Most Chileans prefer traditional tea to coffee, while others drink an herbal infusion called *yerba mate* ("YEHR-bah MAH-teh"), made from the leaves of a shrub belonging to the holly berry family. Enjoyed primarily by rural people, *yerba mate* is made by mixing the ground, greenish herb with hot water and drinking it through a *bombilla* ("bom-BEE-yah"), a metal straw with a bulb-shaped filter at the base. The tea container is passed around and everybody drinks from the same straw. Some *bombillas* are beautifully decorated or even made of silver. The tea is taken in small quantities because of its high caffeine content.

EATING OUT IN CHILE

Although Chileans prefer eating at home, they do have a wide variety of restaurants to choose from, at least in the larger cities. Santiago, Valparaíso, and Concepción have everything from fine dining establishments to hamburger places and many typical Chilean restaurants in between. In Santiago, some of the most elegant restaurants have been established in renovated colonial mansions. Many restaurants serve traditional Chilean specialties and seafood. Others offer classic French and Spanish food. Cuisine from neighboring Latin American countries is easily found and there is a growing number of exotic restaurants.

In most cases, the word *restaurante* applies to a place where both good food and good service are provided. This one is at Angelmo harbor, Puerto Montt.

Bars in Chile serve light snacks and drinks. Most pubs sell only alcoholic beverages, although some serve *empanadas* and light sandwiches. *Fuentes de soda* ("foo-EHN-tehs deh SOH-dah"), or soda fountains, serve soft drinks, fruit juices, and beer. *Parilladas* ("pah-ree-YAH-dahs") offer steaks and other food cooked on a charcoal grill. *Confiterías* ("kohn-fee-teh-REE-ahs") are cake shops that also serve coffee and tea. *Cafeterías* and *hosterías* ("ohs-teh-REE-ahs") are simple eateries. Fastfood chains like McDonald's and the local Doggies have sprouted up all over Chile. Seafood eateries abound.

Many Chilean restaurants offer a set meal called a *menú-del-día* ("meh-NEW-dell-DEE-ah") for lunch and dinner. This very economical meal often consists of a hearty soup, a main course of chicken or meat with rice, and dessert. Diners have to pay extra if they want a salad, vegetables, or potatoes to accompany their meal. Waiters, called *garzón* ("gar-SOHN"), expect a 10 percent tip for good service.

When Chileans dine out in a group, one person pays the entire check. Chileans do not share the bill; they call sharing the bill "American treat!"

MEALTIMES AND TYPICAL MEALS

Breakfast time in Chile is between 7 and 9 A.M. The average breakfast

EMPANADAS

4 cups (946 ml) all-purpose flour	1 whole egg, beaten + 1 egg yolk
1 tablespoon baking powder	1¹/₂ (355 ml) cups warm milk
Salt	1 cup (237 ml) melted shortening
2 tablespoons oil	1 pound (454 g) ground beef
1 teaspoon paprika	3 hard-boiled eggs, sliced
4 finely chopped onions	20 black olives
¹/₂ teaspoon each chili powder, cumin, and oregano	40 large raisins

Sift flour with baking powder and salt. Add egg yolk, egg, milk, and shortening. Mix to make a stiff dough. Divide into 20 pieces and flatten each piece into a circle. Set aside. In a frying pan, heat oil with paprika and sauté onions until soft. Add chili powder, cumin, oregano, and salt. Add meat and mix with onions. Cook until meat turns brown. Place a spoonful of the meat stuffing on half of each dough circle. Add sliced egg, raisins, and olives. Fold dough over filling, wet the edge with milk, fold over again, and seal. Bake in a 400°F (204°C) for 40 minutes or until lightly browned.

Among middle- and upper-class families, the lady of the house does not spend much time in the kitchen, because there is a maid to do the cooking and cleaning. And though kitchens in Chile often have every modern convenience, they are often small and not decorated as living and dining rooms are.

consists of toast and instant coffee or tea—no cereal. Some Chileans eat large breakfasts of ham and eggs. Lunch is typically served at about 1 or 1:30 P.M. and goes on until about 3 P.M. It is the largest meal of the day and often consists of a first course of soup or *empanadas*, a main course of seafood, chicken, or a meat stew, side dishes such as vegetables or potatoes, and ice cream and fruit for dessert.

Afternoon tea in Chile is called *once* ("OHN-say"). There are a number of stories on the origin of the name *once*. Some say that it comes from the British custom of having "elevenses"—a short tea break taken at around 11 A.M.— *(once* means "eleven"). Others attribute it to the miners who, though not allowed to consume alcohol in the mines, secretly added *aguardiente* to their tea; since there are 11 letters in *aguardiente*, it is said that miners began referring to their afternoon "tea" as *once*.

Like Europeans, Chileans dine very late. During the week, dinner is served between 8 and 9 P.M.; on weekends, after 9 P.M. At dinner parties, the meal is often served as late as 10 P.M. Dinner food is similar to lunch food and is followed by coffee or herbal tea. Wine and beer are often served.

TABLE AND PARTY ETIQUETTE

Chileans may not be as formal as other Latin Americans, but they do follow certain rules at the table and in social gatherings. When asked to a dinner party, it is appropriate to arrive about 15 minutes late. If asked for cocktails, the guest will probably be asked to stay for dinner as well. The host and hostess will be sent flowers before the event or given chocolates or whiskey at the party itself. Wine is not a proper gift because it is so plentiful and inexpensive in Chile.

At a formal gathering, it is considered rude to eat anything, even typical

"finger food," using the hands. At sit-down dinners, maids serve each guest a full plate of food. Buffets are also common. Good manners require one to eat a little of everything on the plate, even if some of the food is not to one's liking. When serving wine to someone nearby at a dinner party, the bottle must be held in the right hand.

Often, maids will clear away the dishes and clean up, so it is improper to offer to help. When the meal is over, it is important to spend time talking to and thanking the host and hostess before saying goodbye. Thank-you notes are not necessary in Chile, but a short telephone call is made the day after the party.

PASTEL DE CHOCLO (CORN AND MEAT PIE)

The following two recipes serve 12.

Kernels from 6 ears of corn, grated
8 leaves of finely chopped fresh basil
1 teaspoon salt
3 tablespoons butter
$1/2$ -1 (118–237 ml) cup milk
4 large onions, chopped
3 tablespsoons oil
1 pound (456 g) finely ground lean beef

Salt and pepper to taste
1 teaspoon ground cumin
4 hard-boiled eggs, sliced
1 cup (237 g) raisins
12 pieces of chicken, browned in hot oil, seasoned with salt, pepper and cumin
2 tablespoons confectioners' sugar

Heat the corn kernels, chopped basil, salt and butter in a large pot. Add milk slowly, stirring constantly until the mixture thickens. Cook over low heat for 5 minutes. Set aside. Fry the onions in oil until they are transparent. Add the ground meat and stir till brown. Season with salt, pepper, and ground cumin. To prepare the pie, use an oven-proof dish that you can take to the table. Spread the ground meat mixture over the bottom of the dish. Arrange the hard-boiled egg slices, olives and raisins over the mixture. Put the chicken pieces on top; bone the chicken first if you like. Cover the filling with the corn mixture. Sprinkle the confectioners' sugar over the top. Bake in a hot oven at 400°F (205 °C) for 30-35 minutes until the crust is golden brown. Serve at once.

CAZUELA DE AVE

2 chickens, boned
8 potatoes cut in half
$1/2$ onion
$1/2$ pepper cut in ribbons
7 cups (1.7 l) cold water
1 celery stalk
1 teaspoons oregano
2 heaped tablespoons of rice

1 cup (257 ml) pumpkin seeds
Oil
Salt and pepper

Cut chickens in bite-size pieces. Add oil to a cooking pot and fry chickens in normal heat. Add onions and sauté. Add pepper, celery, oregano, and water. Bring to a boil and cook for about 15 minutes. Add potatoes and rice, turn down heat, cover with lid, and simmer for 20 minutes. Soften pumpkin seeds with a little bit of broth and add seeds to pot. Serve hot.

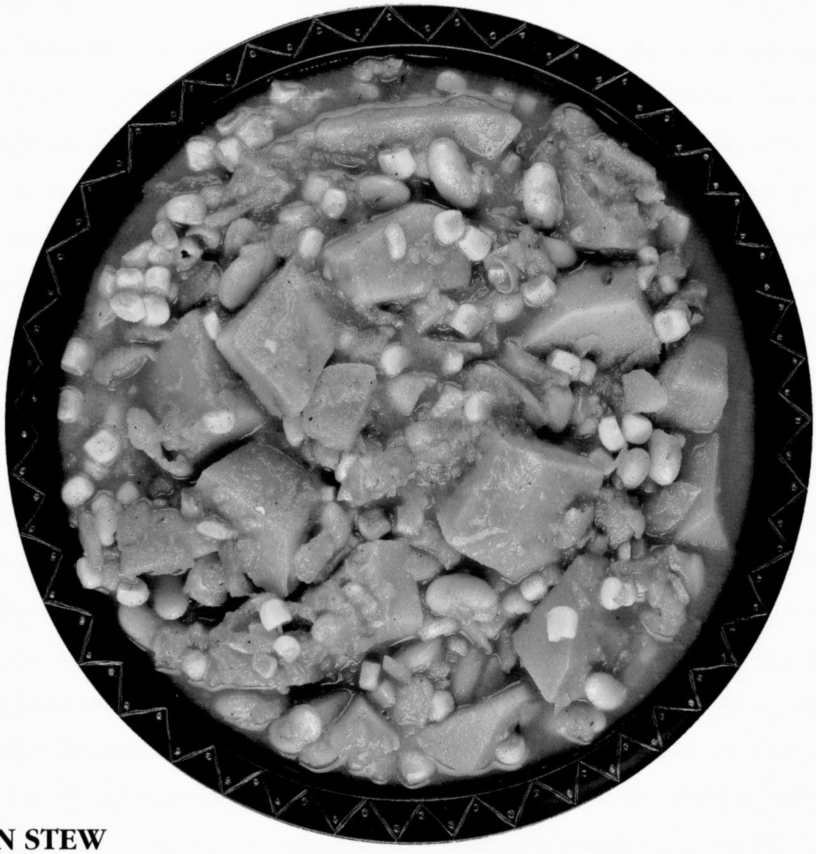

PUMPKIN STEW

This recipe serves six.

3 tablespoons olive oil
2 tablespoons sweet paprika
1 finely chopped onion
4 chopped tomatoes
$1/_2$ teaspoon oregano

Salt and pepper
15-ounce (425 g) can french-cut green beans,
  rinsed and drained
1 pound (453 g) peeled and
  cubed pumpkin
1 cup (237 g) corn, canned or frozen

Heat the oil in a large casserole dish. Stir in paprika: be careful not to let it burn. When it is blended, lower the heat. Add chopped onions and sauté until tender. Add tomatoes and oregano. Season with salt and pepper to taste. Simmer until thick and well blended. Add beans and pumpkin. Add just enough water to cover the beans. Cover the pan and simmer for 15 minutes. Stir in corn and simmer for another 15 minutes.

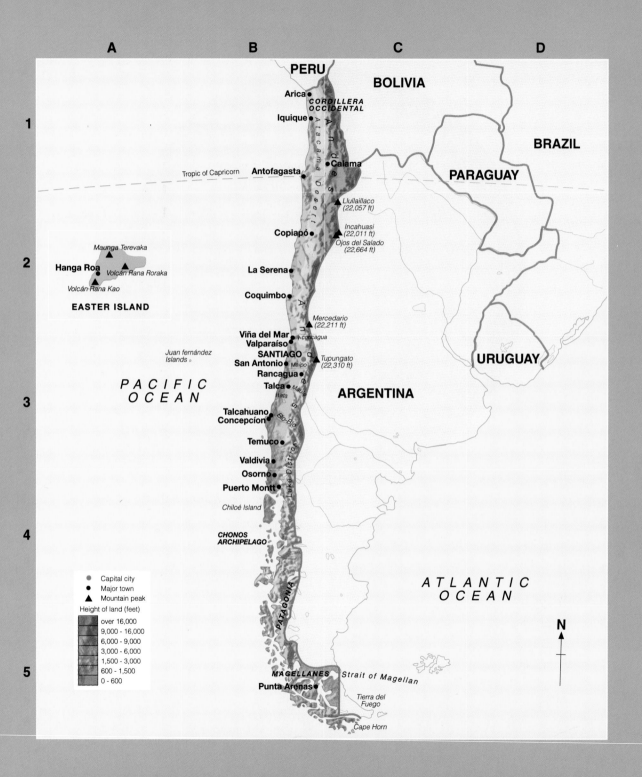

A   **B**   **C**   **D**

PERU

BOLIVIA

Arica•
CORDILLERA OCCIDENTAL

1

Iquique•

BRAZIL

•Calama

PARAGUAY

Tropic of Capricorn
Antofagasta•

▲ Llullaillaco
(22,057 ft)

Copiapó•
▲ Incahuasi
(22,011 ft)
Ojos del Salado
(22,664 ft)

2

La Serena•

Maunga Terevaka ▲

Hanga Roa •
Volcán Rana Roraka ▲

Volcán Rana Kao ▲

Coquimbo•

EASTER ISLAND

Mercedario ▲
(22,211 ft)

Viña del Mar•
Valparaíso•
Aconcagua

Juan fernández
Islands

SANTIAGO
San Antonio•
Rancagua•

Tupungato ▲
(22,310 ft)

URUGUAY

*PACIFIC
OCEAN*

Maipo

Talca•

Maule

3

Itata

ARGENTINA

Talcahuano•
Concepcíon•

Bío-Bío

Temuco•

Valdivia•

Osorno•

Puerto Montt•

Lake District

Chiloé Island

4

*CHONOS
ARCHIPELAGO*

*ATLANTIC
OCEAN*

PATAGONIA

• Capital city
• Major town
▲ Mountain peak
Height of land (feet)

over 16,000
9,000 - 16,000
6,000 - 9,000
3,000 - 6,000
1,500 - 3,000
600 - 1,500
0 - 600

N

5

MAGELLANES
Strait of Magellan
Punta Arenas•

*Tierra del
Fuego*

Cape Horn

MAP OF CHILE

ECONOMIC CHILE

Natural Resources

- Animal Products
- Fishing
- Forestry
- Mining

Agriculture

- Dairy Products
- Fruit
- Grape brandy
- Wine

Services

- **DUTY FREE** Duty Free Zone
- Financial Center
- Port
- Tourism

ABOUT THE ECONOMY

GDP
US$70.2 billion (2001)

GDP SECTORS
Agriculture 8.4 percent, industry and manufacturing 34.2 percent, and services 57.4 percent (2000)

TOURIST ARRIVALS
2 million (2000) per year

LAND AREA
292,257 square miles (756,942 square km)

WORKFORCE
5.9 million (2000)
Professional/technical 10.1 percent; management/administration 3.2 percent; office 14.2 percent; sales 12.6 percent; agriculture; fishing; and ranching 14.3 percent; drivers 5.8 percent; skilled crafts/machinists 19.9 percent; laborers 5.6 percent; personal services 13.3 percent; others 1.0 percent

UNEMPLOYMENT RATE
8.8 percent (January–March 2001)

CURRENCY
1 Chilean peso (Ch$) = 100 centavos
US$1 = 695.35 Ch$ (Oct 2001)
Notes: 500, 1000, 2000, 5000, 10000, 20000
Coins: 1, 5, 10, 50, 100, 500

AGRICULTURAL PRODUCTS
Apples, beans, beef, fish, fruit, grapes, poultry, sugar beets, timber, wheat, wine, and wool

MAJOR EXPORTS
Cellulose, ceramics, copper, fishmeal, fresh fruit, wood, and wood products

MAJOR IMPORTS
Chemicals, electronics, machinery, oil, tools, vehicles, and vehicle parts

MAIN TRADING PARTNERS
United States, European Union, Japan, Argentina, Brazil, and Mexico

INFLATION RATE
4.5 percent (2000)

POVERTY RATE
21.7 percent (1998)

PORTS AND HARBORS
Antofagasta, Arica, Chañaral, Coquimbo, Iquique, Puerto Montt, Punta Arenas, San Antonio, San Vicente, Talcahuano, and Valparaíso

LEADING FOREIGN INVESTORS
United States, Canada, Spain, United Kingdom, Australia, and Japan

CHILEAN INVESTMENT ABROAD
US$6.4 billion
9.4 percent of GDP (1999)

CULTURAL CHILE

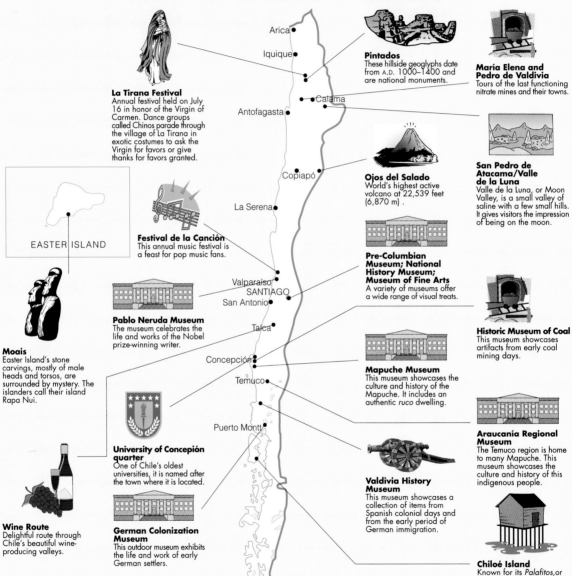

La Tirana Festival
Annual festival held on July 16 in honor of the Virgin of Carmen. Dance groups called Chinos parade through the village of La Tirana in exotic costumes to ask the Virgin for favors or give thanks for favors granted.

EASTER ISLAND

Festival de la Canción
This annual music festival is a feast for pop music fans.

Moais
Easter Island's stone carvings, mostly of male heads and torsos, are surrounded by mystery. The islanders call their island Rapa Nui.

Pablo Neruda Museum
The museum celebrates the life and works of the Nobel prize-winning writer.

University of Concepión quarter
One of Chile's oldest universities, it is named after the town where it is located.

Wine Route
Delightful route through Chile's beautiful wine-producing valleys.

German Colonization Museum
This outdoor museum exhibits the life and work of early German settlers.

Arica
Iquique
Calama
Antofagasta
Copiapó
La Serena
Valparaíso
SANTIAGO
San Antonio
Talca
Concepción
Temuco
Puerto Montt
Punta Arenas

Pintados
These hillside geoglyphs date from A.D. 1000–1400 and are national monuments.

María Elena and Pedro de Valdivia
Tours of the last functioning nitrate mines and their towns.

Ojos del Salado
World's highest active volcano at 22,539 feet (6,870 m) .

San Pedro de Atacama/Valle de la Luna
Valle de la Luna, or Moon Valley, is a small valley of saline with a few small hills. It gives visitors the impression of being on the moon.

Pre-Columbian Museum; National History Museum; Museum of Fine Arts
A variety of museums offer a wide range of visual treats.

Historic Museum of Coal
This museum showcases artifacts from early coal mining days.

Mapuche Museum
This museum showcases the culture and history of the Mapuche. It includes an authentic *ruco* dwelling.

Araucania Regional Museum
The Temuco region is home to many Mapuche. This museum showcases the culture and history of this indigenous people.

Valdivia History Museum
This museum showcases a collection of items from Spanish colonial days and from the early period of German immigration.

Chiloé Island
Known for its *Palafitos,* or houses built on stilts over the water with boats anchored underneath at low tide. Also known for distinct wooden churches built in the 18th and 19th centuries, many of which are national monuments.

Torres del Paine National Park
This park offers a spectacular hiking circuit.

ABOUT THE CULTURE

OFFICIAL NAME
Republic of Chile

CAPITAL
Santiago

OTHER MAJOR CITIES
Antofagasta, Arica, Concepción, Iquique, Puerto Montt, Temuco, Valparaíso, and Viña del Mar

FLAG
Divided into half; the lower half is red, and the upper half has a white star in a blue square on the hoist side. These traditionally "republican" colors are also often interpreted as the blue of the ocean, the white of the Andean snow, and the red of the blood shed for independence. The five-pointed star is a Mapuche symbol.

POPULATION
15 million (2000), 39 percent of which live in the Santiago metropolitan region

ETHNIC GROUPS
Primarily Spanish and *mestizo* with German, Croatian, Palestinian, English, French, Italian, and Jewish. Recent immigration of Koreans.

LIFE EXPECTANCY
75.7 years (2000)

TIME
Greenwich Mean Time minus 4 hours (GMT - 0400)

RELIGIONS
Roman Catholic 80 percent, Protestant 10 percent, others 4 percent

NATIONAL FLOWER
Copihue, a red or pink bell-shaped flower from the lily family.

NATIONAL DANCE
Cueca. A man and woman dance back and forth and around each other, waving handkerchiefs over their heads.

OFFICIAL LANGUAGE
Spanish

LITERACY RATE
94.6 percent (2000)

IMPORTANT ANNIVERSARY
Fiestas Patrias: Independence Day on Sep 18

LEADERS IN SPORTS
Marcelo "El Chino" Rios, tennis player; Ivan "Bam Bam" Zamorano and Marcelo "Matador" Salas, soccer players

TIME LINE

IN CHILE	IN THE WORLD

8000–1000 B.C.
The Chinchorro settle near Arica; these hunter-gatherers mummify their dead in sand.

753 B.C.
Rome is founded.

116–17 B.C.
The Roman Empire reaches its greatest extent, under Emperor Trajan (98-17 B.C.).

A.D. 200–300
The Mapuche begin to develop; Diaguita culture flourishes.

A.D. 600
Height of Mayan civilization

1470–1535
The Incas invade Chile; their empire stretches 155 miles (250 km) south of Santiago.

1000
The Chinese perfect gunpowder and begin to use it in warfare.

1520
Ferdinand Magellan passes through the Straits of Chile that now bears his name.

1530
Beginning of trans-Atlantic slave trade organized by Portuguese in Africa

1535
Diego de Almagro becomes the first European to set foot in Chile.

1541
Pedro de Valdivia founded Santiago.

1558–1603
Reign of Elizabeth I of England

1620
Pilgrim Fathers sail the Mayflower to America.

1704
Alexander Selkirk is deserted on Robinson Crusoe Island for 4 years.

1722
Easter Island is discovered on Easter Sunday by Jacob Roggeveen of Holland.

1776
The U. S. Declaration of Independence

1789–1799
The French Revolution

1810
First autonomous government established.

1814
Spain retakes Chile.

1817
Combined Chilean and Argentinean forces led by José de San Martín defeat Spanish troops.

IN CHILE	IN THE WORLD
1818 Bernardo O'Higgins declares independence.	
1830–1860 Rule of "authoritarian" presidents	**1861** The U.S. Civil War begins.
	1869 The Suez Canal is opened.
1879–1883 War of the Pacific. Chile defeats the Peru-Bolivia confederation.	
1891 Chilean Civil War	**1914** World War I begins.
	1939 World War II begins.
1945 Gabriela Mistral wins Nobel prize in literature.	**1945** The United States drops atomic bombs on Hiroshima and Nagasaki.
1949 Women gain the right to vote in national elections.	**1949** The North Atlantic Treaty Organization (NATO) is formed.
1960 A major earthquake and tsunami hit southern Chile.	**1957** The Russians launch Sputnik.
	1966–1969 The Chinese Cultural Revolution
1970 Salvador Allende is elected president.	
1971 Pablo Neruda wins Nobel prize in literature.	
1973 A military coup overthrows Allende. General Augusto Pinochet heads the military junta.	**1986** Nuclear power disaster at Chernobyl in Ukraine
1990 Patricio Aylwin becomes the first democratically elected president since Allende.	**1991** Break-up of Soviet Union
	1997 Hong Kong is returned to China.
1998 General Pinochet is arrested in England for human rights crimes.	
2000 Ricardo Lagos becomes the first socialist president since Allende.	**2001** World population surpasses 6 billion.

GLOSSARY

aguardiente ("ah-gwarh-dee-EHN-teh")
A very strong alcoholic drink (nearly 70 percent alcohol) distilled from grapes.

arpillera ("ahr-pee-YEH-rah")
A quilt of everyday scenes, originally with a political message.

bombilla ("bom-BEE-yah")
A metal straw with a bulb-shaped filter at the bottom that keeps out the leaves of the *yerba mate* ("YEHR-bah MAH-teh").

camanchaca ("kah-mahn-CHAH-kah")
Extremely humid fog that rolls over the Andes from the ocean.

cartonero ("kahr-toh-NEH-roh")
Someone who rides a bicycle through the streets at night and sorts through garbage for paper or cardboard to sell for recycling.

chueca ("CHWAY-kah")
A well-loved game played by the Mapuche Indians, similar to field hockey.

Concertación ("kohn-sehr-tah-see-OHN")
A political union of center- and left-wing democratic parties.

cueca ("KWAY-kah")
Chile's national folk dance.

empanada ("emh-pah-NAH-dah")
A popular Chilean pastry stuffed with cheese, seafood or meat, with chopped hard-boiled egg, raisins, and olives.

hacienda ("ah-see-EHN-dah")
A farm or ranch.

huaso ("WAH-soh")
A Chilean horseman or cowboy.

la fiesta huasa ("lah fee-EHS-tah WAH-sah")
Chile's rodeo.

manta ("MAHN-tah")
A poncho worn by *huasos*.

once ("OHN-say")
Chilean afternoon tea.

poblaciones ("poh-blah-see-OH-nehs")
Low-income neighborhoods.

porotos granados ("poh-ROH-tohs grah-NAH-doss")
A bean stew.

Restricción ("rehs-treek-see-OHN")
A government policy to help reduce pollution in Santiago. Between March and December, cars without catalytic converters are prohibited from driving one day a week.

santiaguinos ("sahn-tee-ah-GEE-nohs")
Residents of Santiago.

soroche ("soh-ROH-chay")
Mountain or altitude sickness.

tonada ("toh-NAH-dah")
A sentimental ballad.

FURTHER INFORMATION

BOOKS

Arriaza, Bernardo T. and John W. Verano. *Beyond Death: The Chinchorro Mummies of Ancient Chile*. Washington, D.C.: Smithsonian Institute Press, 1995.

Beccaceci, Marcelo D. *Natural Patagonia/Patagonia Natural: Argentina and Chile*. Minnesota: Pangaea, 1998.

Castillo-Feliu, Guillermo I. *Culture and Customs of Chile*. Connecticut: Greenwood, 2000.

Dwyer, Christopher. *Chile*. Major World Nations series. Pennsylvania: Chelsea House, 1997.

Faron, Louis C. *The Mapuche Indians of Chile*. Illinois: Waveland, 1986.

Muller, Karin. *The Incan Road*. Washington, D.C.: Adventure Press/National Geographic, 2000.

Pickering, Marianne. *Chile: Where the Land Ends*. Utah: Benchmark Books, 1997.

Roraff, Susan and Laura Camacho. *Culture Shock! Chile*. Singapore: Times Books International, 2001.

Selby, Anna. *Argentina, Chile, Paraguay and Uruguay: Country Fact File*. Texas: Raintree Steck-Vaughn, 1999.

WEBSITES

American Chamber of Commerce in Chile. www.amchamchile.cl

Central Intelligence Agency World Factbook (select "Chile" from the country list). www.odci.gov/cia/publications/factbook/index.html

Chile Information Project. www.chip.cl

Lonely Planet World Guide: Destination Chile. www.lonelyplanet.com/destinations/south_america/chile_and_easter_island

National Tourism Board of Chile. www.sernatur.cl

VIDEOS

Chile and Easter Island. Lonely Planet, 1997.

Full Circle with Michael Palin: Chile, Bolivia and Peru. PBS Home Video, 1998.

Secrets of the Lost Empires II: Easter Island. WGBH, 2000.

BIBLIOGRAPHY

Box, Ben (editor). *Footprint South American Handbook 2001* (77th edition). Chicago: Passport Books, 2000.

Brosse, Jacques. *Great Voyages of Discovery: Circumnavigators and Scientists 1764–1843*, translated by Stanley Hochman. New York: Facts on File Publications, 1983.

Constable, Pamela and Arturo Valenzuela. *A Nation of Enemies: Chile under Pinochet*. New York: W.W. Norton, 1993.

Devine, Elizabeth, and Nancy L. Braganti. *The Traveler's Guide to Latin American Customs and Manners*, New York: St. Martin's Press, 2000.

Harvey, Robert. *Fire Down Below*, New York: Simon and Schuster, 1988.

Haverstock, Nathan A. *Chile in Pictures*, Minneapolis: Lerner Publications Company, 1999.

Informe Pais: Estado del Medio Ambiente en Chile 1999. Santiago: University of Chile, 1999.

Jacobsen, Karen. *Chile*, Chicago: Children's Press, 1991.

St. John, Jetty. *A Family in Chile*, Minneapolis: Lerner Publications Company, 1986.

INDEX